Piney Woods School

Piney Woods School

An Oral History

By
Alferdteen B. Harrison
With Photographs by Roland Freeman

UNIVERSITY PRESS OF MISSISSIPPI
Jackson

COPYRIGHT © 1982 BY THE UNIVERSITY PRESS OF MISSISSIPPI
ALL RIGHTS RESERVED
MANUFACTURED IN THE UNITED STATES OF AMERICA

Print-on-Demand Edition

*This volume has been sponsored by
Jackson State University*

Library of Congress Cataloging in Publication Data

Harrison, Alferdteen.
  Piney Woods School, an oral history.

  Bibliography: p.
  Includes index.
  1. Piney Woods School—History. 2. Community and school—Mississippi—Braxton. I. Title.
  LC2852.B72H37 1982   371'.03'0976259   82-11150
  ISBN 0-87805-167-8

Contents

	Preface	vii
	Introduction	3
1	A School Comes to Piney Woods	13
2	Education for the Folks	40
3	The Students of Piney Woods	65
4	Support for Growth and Expansion	91
5	The School in a Changing Society	109
6	Past, Present, and Future	133
	Notes	142
	Sources	155
	Index	163

Preface

The history of Piney Woods School offers a remarkable opportunity for the study of political and social change in the rural American South during the twentieth century. In setting forth that history, I have tried to present a balanced view of the school's operations, academic program and goals, relationship with the surrounding community, and evolution during its first seventy years. My aim has not been to evaluate the merits of education at Piney Woods now or in the past or to suggest a means to educational reform elsewhere. Rather, I have sought to place industrial education at Piney Woods in the historical continuum that begins in America with the founding of Hampton and Tuskegee institutes; to document and consider possible reasons for the school's success in the larger community; and to suggest, tentatively, how an educational institution can remain (and has remained) responsive to the changing needs of the times.

This work would not have been possible without the financial assistance of many institutions. I am indebted to the Jackson State University Faculty Research Committee for two research grants that permitted me to interview extensively; to the Advanced Institutional Development Program of the Department of Health, Education, and Welfare for initial support in processing my oral history research; to the Moton Institute's Independent Studies Fellowship Program for salary support and for research and writing facilities; to the National Endowment for the Humanities, Research Division, for final support in completing research and writing; and to the Institute for the Study of

History, Life, and Culture of Black People, Jackson State University, for assistance with revisions.

I have greatly benefited from the insights and ideas shared with me by present and former members of the Piney Woods community, particularly its students, faculty, and administration. Without their help this book might never have existed. I also thank the many students who transcribed and typed my various drafts. I especially appreciate the freedom I was given to use materials from the Piney Woods Archives. All of the photographs in this book, unless otherwise credited, belong to the school archives.

During the research, planning, and writing stages several educators gave me valuable assistance. Some are members of the faculties at Jackson State University and at other universities and professional associations. I thank Joyce Giaquinta, manuscript librarian at the Iowa State Historical Society, and Sylvia Lyons Render of the Library of Congress, Manuscript Division, for the understanding guidance that they provided to their collections.

Piney Woods School

Introduction

Piney Woods School was founded in 1909 with the aim of giving impoverished rural blacks an industrial education. Laurence C. Jones (1882–1975), its founder, recommended that all graduates of his school acquire no fewer than three skills for earning a living. The first skill should be mastered; the other two should be learned well enough so that one of them could be used if the first one failed. Although Jones was himself a product of the liberal arts tradition, he believed that manual labor education could help people on society's bottom rung, or as he put it, the "bottom rail." He said, an "old-time rail fence . . . would fall down, no matter how many good rails were inserted, unless the bottom rail was strong, substantial, and properly placed." Throughout human history there has always been "a bottom rail in every country and every age."[1] Jones's school was successful, as this book shows, and the widespread demand for industrial education today is apparent from the eagerness of students to learn skills that will help them find work.

At the time when Jones was emerging as an advocate of industrial education, the philosophies of W. E. B. DuBois and Booker T. Washington were being widely discussed. Whereas Washington advocated an education for blacks that combined manual labor with academic training, proponents of DuBois's views argued that a "talented tenth" should be educated specifically for leadership of the black race and that improved conditions for blacks generally would result from political agitation.[2] Although the two approaches were not necessarily incompatible, disputes often made them seem so.

Students Rhoda Gaddis (far right) and Wesly Jones (third from right) learn data processing skills by working with administrative staff members (from left) Mary Jo Reynolds, Dr. John B. Jones, and Florence Davis. (Photo courtesy of Roland Freeman)

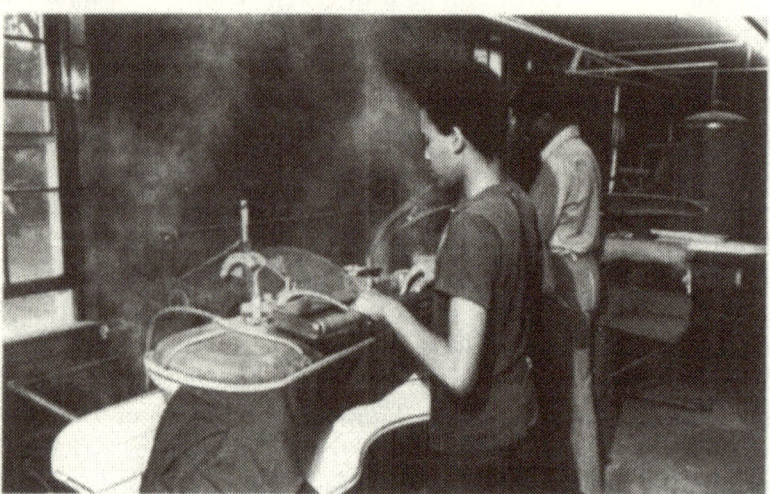

Warren Bowen (left) and Maurice Nicholson work regularly in the school's dry cleaning shop to fulfill their obligations in the school's required work program. (Photo courtesy of Roland Freeman)

The problem of how to educate American blacks in the late nineteenth and early twentieth centuries derived its urgency from the need to integrate large numbers of former slaves into an often hostile white society. In using industrial education to address this need, Piney Woods School was preceded by Hampton and Tuskegee institutes (founded in 1868 and 1881, respectively). In all three schools "industrial education" meant the adaptation of vocational training to the requirements of the pupils and their communities. Important school activities included industrial, agricultural, and household work as well as moral and religious instruction.³ Since students generally lacked the means to pay for their education, industrial capitalists and their supporters often supplied the tuition.

Historian James D. Anderson has charged that Robert C. Ogden, George Foster Peabody, and William Henry Baldwin, the southern industrialists who supported Hampton and Tuskegee, "were more interested in people to propagandize certain political, social, and economic ideas," than in teaching the industrial technology.

> As the slave-owners needed black drivers so did the industrial capitalists need a black manufactured elite to supervise and inform thousands of black workers and channel them into predetermined courses. . . . This economic consideration prompted the philanthropic leaders to provide for a small number of industrial institutes that would produce black industrial leaders. . . . [The industrial lessons were:] "Face the music"; avoid social questions; leave politics alone; continue to be patient; live moral lives; live simply; learn to work intelligently; learn to work faithfully; learn to work hard; learn that any work, however menial, if well done is dignified; . . . learn that it is a mistake to be educated out of your necessary environment; know that it is a crime for any teacher, white or black, to educate the negro for positions which are not open to him."⁴

Various critics have asked whether such educational programs equipped blacks to survive or whether they simply prepared their students for continued subservience. Rather than debate the question, I will consider Piney Woods School as it reflected a

Broommaking was a necessary activity for some students in earlier years. The brooms were sold to produce income for the school.

High school students have an opportunity to acquire automotive mechanic skills. Instructor Jerome Schmidt monitors the progress of (from left) Rollie Carr, Henry Peterson, and Lynn Adams. (Photo courtesy of Roland Freeman)

philosophy different from that of the liberal arts, or classical, tradition.

Although experiments with industrial education multiplied in Europe with the advent of the Industrial Revolution, the basic theory had been tested with varying results well before the birth of Laurence Jones in 1882 and even before the establishment of Hampton Institute. The notion that schools could train students in manual labor as well as in other, more traditional subjects originated with Johann Heinrich Pestalozzi (1746–1827). As early as 1774 this Swiss educator had won a reputation as the champion of the underprivileged and the exploited. He "established an orphanage where he attempted to teach neglected children the rudiments of agriculture and simple trades that they might lead productive, self-reliant lives." Though the orphanage experiment failed in 1780, by 1805 Pestalozzi had founded a boarding school at Yverdon which stressed "sense impression": "accurate, clear thinking dependent upon accurate observation of actual objects; words and ideas having meaning only when related to concrete things."[5]

An associate of Pestalozzi, Phillip E. von Fellenberg (1771–1844), in 1806 at Hofwyl began combining manual training with agricultural and academic instruction in an effort to improve the living conditions of the poor and to reduce the disparity between the lower and upper classes. Students came to him from all over Europe to study "agriculture and to profit by the high moral training which he associated with the educational system."[6]

Manual labor education was perhaps first used in the United States by Rev. George W. Gale at Western Reserve Theological Seminary in 1826. He took young converts and taught them divinity in his home while they paid for their instruction, books, and board by working on his farm for a certain number of hours each day. He reported on this experiment at the Oneida Presbyter on February 14, 1827.[7] The next well-known American experiment with manual labor education occurred at Oberlin College, beginning about 1833. Here students worked and went to school at the same time. Though there were problems, in the 1840s the experiment seemed promising.

Before the days of coin-operated machines, students working in the school laundry washed and ironed the clothes of Piney Woods faculty members.

Other attempts followed. Laurence Jones's uncle, Prior Foster, organized the Woodstock Manual Labor Institute in Addison, Michigan, in 1846. This was a work-your-way school for both whites and blacks. Integration of academic instruction with manual training next became important at Michigan Agricultural College, founded, in 1855 (it is now Michigan State University).[8] Manual labor education developed here at other agricultural colleges, and the Woodstock Institute closed after the Civil War, when the state of Michigan became responsible for black education. At this time, too, grants of private funds for black education generally shifted south.

By 1868, when Samuel C. Armstrong founded Hampton Institute, the Oberlin experiment had failed. While assessing its failure, Armstrong recalled his childhood days in Hawaii, where he had seen the Hilo Manual Labor School for native Hawaiians. It was a boarding school for boys, who paid their expenses by working in carpentry, housework, gardening, and other chores in which they received some slight instruction. Armstrong concluded that on this model he could design an education for former slaves in the United States. He believed that by working, students would acquire self-respect, self-reliance, and character. Students trained as teachers could return to their homes to help improve living conditions for the betterment of the black community. Hampton's graduates were to work in the South, where there were no agricultural or normal schools for Negroes.[9]

Hampton Institute gave black students a chance to work for their room, board, and tuition; and Armstrong joined the vanguard of those who sought to prepare former slaves for the new social order. He passed his concept of a dual educational purpose on to his student, Booker T. Washington. As a result of Washington's efforts, industrial education became the preeminent means of equipping southern blacks for life as freedmen.

Before the Civil War a few blacks had been informally educated by individual members of slaveholding families. In addition, some philanthropists had freed and educated their slaves, and a few had even sent freedmen abroad for an education. After the war, public financial support for black education developed slowly even in Mississippi, where public schools were established as early as 1870. Some individuals asked whether the masses of former slaves could successfully be taught, and there was even greater concern about how the effort was to be financed. By the time Piney Woods was founded in 1909, much of the educational challenge had been taken up by the volunteer services of the abolitionists.[10]

From 1865 to 1871 abolitionists worked for black education primarily through the Freedman's Bureau and through northern missionary societies. The void left by the bureau's failure in 1871 was partially filled by missionary groups, philanthropic agencies, and federal support. The missionary groups included the American Missionary Society, the American Baptist Home Mission, the African Methodist Episcopal Church, and other institutions that organized and financed schools. The early philanthropic agencies included:

Nearly all the brick buildings constructed at Piney Woods have been built with bricks made by the students. Students in this photograph are making the cement and sand bricks with which the first five brick buildings were built.

1. the Peabody Education Fund, 1867–1914, providing educational opportunities for blacks and whites;
2. the John F. Slater Fund, 1882, for assisting southern blacks;[11]
3. the General Education Board, established in 1902 by John D. Rockefeller for cooperation with public and private educational activities without discrimination (it advocated industrial education for blacks);
4. the Anna T. Jeanes Fund, 1907, for assisting rural Negro schools;
5. the Phelps-Stokes Fund, 1911, to aid black Americans and Africans;
6. the Rosenwald Fund, 1917, for assistance in the construction of school buildings for black children.[12]

The major federal programs included the Morrill Land Grant Acts of 1862 and 1890, the Smith-Lever Act, and the Smith-Hughes Act. Missionary groups, private groups, and government acts significantly aided black educational development. Yet the early twentieth century saw a significant decline in public support for black education that was accompanied by more frequent lynchings, more Jim Crow laws, and more reactionary terrorist groups. To counter such developments the descendants of the slaves increasingly organized their own educational institutions, supported by their churches, secret societies, and Masonic lodges. In the entire state of Mississippi there was not a single accredited public high school in 1909 that blacks could attend, and for years Alcorn College was the sole state-supported institution of higher learning for blacks. It did not supply enough teachers to meet the demand for rural teacher development, however, and a second institution, Jackson College, became state supported, though not until 1940.

Four blacks were inspired to found educational institutions during the period 1903–1926. They were William H. Holtzclaw, who started Utica Institute (1903); J. E. Johnson, Prentiss Institute (1907); Laurence C. Jones, Piney Woods School (1909); and Arena C. Mallory King, Saints Jr. College (1926). The oldest of these schools, Utica and Prentiss, have links to Tuskegee. Holtzclaw was a graduate of Tuskegee, and Utica Institute became known as the "Little Tuskegee" of Mississippi. The cofounders of Prentiss Institute were J. E. Johnson, Sr., a graduate of Alcorn, and his wife, Bertha L. Johnson, a graduate of Tuskegee. Booker T. Washington often recommended Utica and Prentiss institutes for funding grants, and George Washington Carver, the scientist from Tuskegee, visited both schools annually during farmers' conferences. As one black student noted:

> These educators and their schools held black education together until the white power structure saw fit to improve the public school system. If any black got a high school diploma, he had to leave home to get it. . . . He couldn't go anywhere except Piney Woods, Prentiss, or Utica and of course a school in Meridian. At that time Tougaloo, Alcorn, and Jackson colleges had high school departments. But they were money schools. Piney Woods, Utica and Prentiss gave students a chance to work their way through school.[13]

Industrial education at these institutions found acceptance despite the hostile racial climate, meeting the desperate need for schooling for the rural folk. The following chapters describe the history of Piney Woods School, including its educational goals, instructional program, relationship with the surrounding community, and financial support, as well as the social forces which fostered change.

I

A School Comes to Piney Woods

> *Imagine the dense pine woods of a state in the deep South, flavor the air with the scent of old pines and of rough pine lumber, listen for bird-calls and the ringing of tools all day long. . . . So thick are the woods that the school can hardly be seen from a hill a mile away.**

The Rankin County Piney Woods region, in which the Piney Woods Country Life School was located, was considered to have the poorest land, cattle, and people. As a result, in 1909 the name "Piney Woods" was often used derisively. For Jones, however, the words beautifully described the area. Later, however, reflecting on his choice of name, he wrote, "It was as though we had chosen to christen a baby 'useless' or to name a stately mansion 'shanty.' "[1]

The school was located in the sparsely populated northwest edge of the region, forty-two miles southeast of Jackson, Mississippi, where tall pine trees with long needles rise from sandy soil. This land, together with the Jackson Prairie in the northern two-thirds of the county and the Loess Hills to the southwest, has made Rankin a place of great poverty, in stark contrast to the rich, fertile soil of northwestern Mississippi's Delta. Because land was cheap, it was settled by families who could not afford

---

*Mary Jenness in "A Homemade School in the Deep South," *Twelve Negro Americans*, 102–103.

acreage in the Delta, particularly in the Natchez region. The white inhabitants of the Piney Woods area, who came from the Carolinas and Georgia, are known even today for their personal honesty and simple hospitality. In contrast to the planter class of the Natchez area they were not aristocratic or intellectual, nor were they usually educated in the eastern colleges or abroad.[2]

The small number of white pioneers who settled in the Piney Woods made a living from lumbering, commerce, and small farms. When the Indians ceded lands in north Mississippi, settlers who could afford to do so departed to buy farms farther north. Those who remained could not afford slaves, and most of the population of the Piney Woods thus remained white. In 1837 the population of Rankin County was 3,255 whites and 1,956 slaves.

During the Civil War residents of Piney Woods gained a reputation for disloyalty to the Confederacy. "The Pearl River counties, being well provided with swamps, were a haven to deserters, who—as elsewhere in the Piney Woods—banded together under the Federal flag, set patrols along the roads and proceeded to destroy ginhouses and ferries."[3] R. A. McLemore has concluded that "Unionism" among settlers in the hills and swamps probably described merely backwoods resistance to interference with an independent life-style. (At one time inhabitants of the region had been known to shoot federal revenue officials.)

In spite of its pro-Union tendencies during the Civil War, this area of Mississippi afforded blacks opportunities little better than those in any other part of the state. John R. Webster, a white native of the area and the owner of the local Comby Saw Mill, recalled living in about 1885 on the old Braxton and Westville Road eighteen miles from the railroad. According to the oral tradition of that community, prior to 1857 "there was a colony of negroes just north of us on a sixteenth section of land and some railroad land, some old land that had been abandoned by the white settler." The soil was hilly and poor. Former slaves picked the location "because of its cheapness, and it was known around about as Free Town."⁴ Webster recalled most of the families of the area—those of Ed Campbell, Montague Harris, Nathan Taylor, Alex McLaurin, and many others. As a child he played with many blacks, including Steve Cox and the McLaurins. He recalled that the families of former slaves

> had to start from taw. Their houses were pole shanties. They would plow a little ox. Some of them had a little pony. Their tools were mostly home made, wood plow stocks, wood harrows with wood teeth. The men would clear, build and fence. The women would travel out and work for white ladies in the adjoining settlements, for a little meal, molasses, or old clothes, or they would hire out a young son of good plow[ing] age to some planter on the creek and bottom lands for $7.50 a month. This would help the family pull through.⁵

There were no arrests or violations of laws at the time. Webster also recalled Montague Harris's forty acres and pole shanty "just a mile from my house. He plowed a little spotted ox and had about fifteen acres cleared. He got his water from a large spring on the place. He planted an umbrella china in his yard for shade. We children would go there for berries to shoot in our pop guns. Uncle Montague was always jolly with us."⁶ Piney Woods School was eventually founded on Harris's land.

Despite Webster's positive childhood recollections, the freedman's position in the white world was perilous. Grounds for offense were broadly construed, and penalties were severe. As Webster noted, "the psychology of the people was the result of tradition and the impressions of slavery. The inferiority of the slave and the superiority of the master wouldn't give away to common justice. So the Negro had no standing in society, schools, or courts of laws."⁷ Webster was more able than most blacks or whites to understand the political reality that trapped both races within the confines of their heritage.

Because of the prevailing social and political climate, no school for blacks could have thrived in the Piney Woods without the support of the white community. Laurence Jones cultivated such support in Braxton, the nearest town, in Simpson County,

A view of Braxton, Mississippi, in 1909, the year Laurence Jones founded Piney Woods Country Life School on a forty-acre plot nearby.

Mississippi. About 75 percent of Braxton's population was white and about 25 percent black; according to B. T. McCullough, the present mayor, blacks lived on the outer edges of Braxton, as they do today, but never in or near the central part of town.[8]

Braxton was founded in 1885 and was a cotton center with a gin and several stores as well as several logging communities on its periphery. When the Gulf and Ship Island Railroad arrived in 1900, several sawmills began to operate in the area, shipping lumber out by rail. The advent of a lumbering boom in the Piney Woods altered the antebellum image of white poverty and created attitudes that fostered the growth of Piney Woods School. There was no great demand for unskilled labor, as there was in the Mississippi Delta, and white people in the Piney Woods were therefore more receptive to a school that would better prepare black laborers for work.[9]

The parents of some early students were sharecroppers and tenant farmers. Some were public workers who cut and hauled logs at Belpine, Comby, Cohay, and other sawmills or even

Leola Hughes (1892–), a life-long resident of Rankin County, was one of the first students to attend Piney Woods. (Photo courtesy of Roland Freeman)

worked in the logging camps, cutting and hauling the timber to the mills or to the train station in Braxton.[10] Others struggled as subsistence farmers or as domestic workers, hoping and praying for a better day. One writer in 1936 described the blacks' dwellings as "nests of log cabins [hidden in the woods], many of which were built by slaves before the Civil War and are today inhabited by their descendants, practically slaves themselves under the sharecropping system of tenantry."[11]

A fuller (and more vivid) account of living conditions at the time when Piney Woods School was founded is provided by the statements of the blacks themselves. The family of Leola Hughes owned their farm, as did fewer than 5 percent of black farmers in the area. At age eighty-one Mrs. Hughes spoke of the family tradition of "proving" up the land in the Piney Woods on the Rankin side of the Simpson County line.

> I'm just one mile from the county line of Rankin and Simpson. My uncle was old man Elijah Campbell, an ex-slave man. Him and his wife raised my mother. Practically all the land right round in this

settlement . . . from here to Piney Woods School was owned by Steven Crawford, who used to live up in Madison County near Tougaloo, where they were living on white folks' land. This land around here was government land.[12] You could move on it and improve it. Say, cut down enough logs if you fixin' to build a lumber house, and a mighty few people could at that time. Have been a time where every house around here was a log house, 'cause too many of us couldn't build a lumber house. Most of this land was bought up right here—in this settlement, here—by colored folks, and they homesteaded. My uncle homesteaded sixty acres. He cut down some poles and built him a little old shack to live in it the best way he could. After so many years, they do what they called "proving it up." He said when he got through proving up that sixty acres, he paid sixteen dollars . . . at the Court House in Brandon. There was my uncle, Elijah Campbell, Ed Taylor, Ed Crawford, and Steven Crawford and Andy Lunford. They all homestead this land in Rankin County, not in Simpson County.[13]

Like many of the other farmers, black and white, the Hugheses were trapped in a subsistence-level economy.

Mrs. Rosie Brooks's father purchased some land to the north of the school. When she was a student at Piney Woods, she recalled, the Webster sawmill in the Comby community was

right where the dairy barn is, kind of close to the railroad. They had a big sawmill there. My father cut logs all through this community clean on back near Pellahatchie for years. He cut this timber off this land about three times. If it growed up, he'd get that. . . . That's the way he paid for his forty acres of land down here, bu out sawing logs.

And mama would take us children and make crops. And they bought the forty acres of land we lived on after they got tired of renting, you know, having to move from place to place. As we growed up, he said, well, "I'm tired of dragging my wife and my children from farm to farm." He said, "I'm gonna get out and work and buy me some land of my own . . . and that's what he did. He bought forty acres of land . . . from the Brandon Bank.[14]

Steve and Nellie Cox, parents of Mrs. Brooks, were influenced by Piney Woods School to become landowners instead of renters. Such families succeeded in leaving dwellings that

Nellie Cox (1884–1980) provided a place for Jones to stay when he first came to Piney Woods. (Photo courtesy of Roland Freeman)

Jones, recalling his early students, described as "often the most humble log cabins far away from the main traveled roads. . . . in them the only books visible were the Bible and perhaps a *Sears Roebuck* or *Montgomery Ward* catalogue."[15]

Mrs. Deborah Gray Polk, a former home demonstration worker and Piney Woods student (1920–1924), recalled that the community around Piney Woods was rough. "Most all the homes out there were just [made out of] logs—maybe just a two-room house, one room and maybe a little kitchen to it. And some of the people cooked on the outside. They had these things they call ovens. They looked like old-fashioned wash pots with long handles. Food was put into them. Then they'd put the coals on top, and the food would cook."[16]

Although their lives showed some common patterns, black people used a variety of tactics in their struggle to survive. According to Mrs. Hughes,

> My people were farmers and my mother would have to work in the field and help gather the crop. So in the wintertime when it was cold and we'd have a little breathing spell, well, she'd just sit around a big log-heaped fire and make quilts. She'd have all those quilt tops pieced up that she pieced during the winter. She was a woman [who] had to do something all the time.
>
> I wanted to piece quilts, and I cried and hollered, and my daddy told her, say, "give that child some quilt scraps. If she wants to piece quilts, let her have it." I started to piecing up a quilt, and I think I was about twelve before I got enough. But I pieced that quilt and me and her quilted it. When I first started sitting down at them frames and started to quilting, I was quilting on my own quilt. I was the proudest little girl that I had a quilt hanging up in the frame, quilting on it.
>
> When I was a kid, you could buy good cloth for four cents a yard. My mother used to buy whole boards of it to make up work clothes. All that she didn't use she'd put in quilts. I cut out and made my first dress when I was thirteen.[17]

Jones observed the Piney Woods families as an outsider and described them as a community.

> Their philosophy of life was to get something to eat, and to make their farm enable them to live. Every man was very happy if he had

a hog in a pen that would make him meat for the winter. They were very happy to raise more vegetables than they could eat, so that they could can some of the things or dry them. About that time the government county agent was encouraging people to can things and to have good gardens. About the only philosophy of life that the people had in Piney Woods in that day was to make a living that would enable them to enjoy life.

To enjoy life was to go to town on Saturday and meet their friends and chat with them, and to go to some church on Sunday. Those are the things that they enjoyed and they didn't read many newspapers, so church would be a place where they could pass the time of day and discuss the events of the week. Strangers would often wonder why they would be outside of the church after it was over such a long time. But that was the only opportunity that they had to discuss things and to try to decide things that needed any decision in regard to the church or otherwise. So they visited and enjoyed life just as people in the cities had their club meetings and things of that kind.[18]

Such recollections make possible greater understanding of the impact that Piney Woods School had in its immediate vicinity.

Of the more than 30,000 blacks in the Piney Woods area, 50 percent were illiterate. The lack of educational opportunities became almost absolute when Gov. James Vardaman "abolished the only Negro Normal School in the state with the explanation that 'Negro education is a threat to white supremacy.'"[19] Piney Woods School was founded during Vardaman's tenure in office.

Though the school was just (and is) inside the Rankin County line, it also served Simpson to the south and Scott and Smith counties on the east. For many years Piney Woods was the only graded industrial school in this area. According to the 1900 census, the population included 8,679 whites and 12,276 blacks.[20] This population had somewhat increased by 1906, when the white schools in the county numbered sixty-four and the black schools fifty-five. The school term usually lasted six months. White legislators and government officials held that there was not enough money to support both black and white school systems adequately. The white school officials reasoned that since blacks owned little property, their taxes were insufficient for their educational support. Separate, but not equal, facilities for blacks seemed justifiable to the white community. Few people believed that every child in the Mississippi backwoods was entitled to a real education, especially in the regions with poor land, where wealth was measured in horses.

As one writer observed, "the average rural school for colored people was generally back in the woods far from the main traveled roads." It was "unsealed, without windows, no blackboards, charts or maps." Schools like Piney Woods offered 90 percent of blacks their only chance for education above the fifth or eighth grades. In Rankin County not a single high school for blacks went beyond the fifth grade when Piney Woods was started, and the existing schools set educational standards, even for the early grades, that were lower than those of most public schools in other states. Jones observed, most of the "teachers did not measure up to fifth grade boys and girls of an Iowa school."[21] Perhaps Piney Woods' most important contribution to the community consisted in improving the quality of available educational opportunities, an achievement that was certainly due to Jones's efforts.

Laurence Clifton Jones was born into an integrated Jewish and German community in St. Joseph, Missouri, on November 21, 1882. As a black youth he attended a segregated public elementary school. He spent many hours reading in the public library, attended the Episcopal church and, showing enterprise at any early age, raised chickens and pigeons for trade or sale. His first jobs away from home included shining shoes at a barber shop; passing out cups of water at the local theater; delivering newspapers; and shaking out bales of excelsior at a mattress factory.[22]

Laurence admired his father, John Jones, for his self-confidence, his strength, and his service in the army from 1867 to 1876. A tall, striking Afro-Castilian from El Paso, Texas, John Jones had begun his working career as a drayman with a pair of goats in Alabama. Later he became head porter and owner of the barber shop at the Pacific Hotel, where Laurence often accompanied him, and at one time he also owned a summer cottage and some rental properties.[23]

Social advancement figured importantly in John Jones's expectations for his son. Laurence learned that his childhood savings were meant to help him attend college or start work, perhaps by buying a span of mules. If Laurence did not go to college, in short, he should prepare to make himself useful—to do something that would put him "'ahead of the old generation.'"[24]

Though John Jones made a comfortable living for his family, his wife, Mary Foster Jones, was an excellent seamstress who sewed by the day. Before she met John Jones, she had owned a sewing shop with her sister in Marysville, Missouri. After her marriage her sewing enabled her to purchase a few extra frills for the home. Jobs sewing and serving took her away from the home often. During her absences, Aunt Eliza, a neighbor, tended the house and cared for Laurence and his sisters Ruby Ethel and Flora Mae, who died at an early age (another sister, Nellie Elaine, was born much later). Aunt Eliza was a spiritual influence in Jones's life and reinforced his mother's teachings.

Mary Foster was born in Wisconsin to free-born parents who had migrated from Virginia by way of Ohio. She was a fragile quadroon who believed in neatness and regarded a job well done as a daily duty to God. She expected Laurence to be like his father, and she taught him to emulate all of the prominent men of his race. She also commended to him certain traits of his ancestors, particularly her great grandfather, Robert Foster, who during the Revolutionary period had purchased his freedom in Virginia and had moved to Pennsylvania, where he married a Pennsylvania Dutch woman, Rebecca Bilmyer. Laurence's own grandfather, Robert Foster, had four sons who were well educated and had probably benefited from the Underground Railway. One of these men, Prior Foster, moved from Ohio to Michigan, where he founded the Woodstock Manual Labor Institute in 1846. It became a family project. Prior Foster's brother in Wisconsin sent money annually, and once or twice he sent wagons of corn and produce.[25] "Once a year Foster would go east to solicit funds and make friends for the race."[26] Later this family educational tradition was reflected in the relationship that Piney Woods established with its community.

At the age of sixteen, in the fall of 1898, Laurence Jones found the St. Joseph High School curriculum unrelated to practical living. Without telling his parents, he purchased a ticket, hid his books under the railroad bridge, and went to live with relatives first in Illinois and later in Iowa. As a high school student in Marshalltown, Iowa, he tutored a black girl who could not attend school because she had scrofula on her neck. Before her death he had prepared her for the second reader and had taught her to do practical problems in arithmetic, such as totaling the cost of items at the store and making change.

As the first black graduate from Marshalltown High School in 1903, Jones received a scholarship to the University of Iowa. His application read: "I am making my own way through school and am hungry for a thorough education which I intend using in the great work of helping to elevate my race in the south."[27] His commitment was particularly reinforced during his college years, when he heard the university president, George E. McLean, use the phrase *noblesse oblige*.

The most significant intellectual experience of this period which reinforced Jones's deepening commitment to the black people of the South was his detailed study of the industrial arts movement with his English professor, Clarke Fisher Ansley (1869–1939). From his research, Jones recalled, he began to see where the Industrial Arts Movement "was coming into being in the world . . . and I felt that . . . if a Negro caught on to the . . . movement he would be able to accomplish a great deal to help . . . his development."[28] He looked to Hampton and Tuskegee institutes as models. "I became so saturated with their ideals and accomplishments that by way of testimony to my enthusiasm, I was given the entire class period for a week in which to report on them. The allotted time for reports from each student was usually only one hour."[29]

A local university town newspaper, the *Iowa Citizen*, on Monday, May 7, 1906, carried an article entitled, "Jones Speaks on Tuskegee." It reported that Jones

> showed by statistics that the southern negro schools were more than supported by taxes paid by the negro people. He emphasized the fact that Tuskegee was not a servant's training school but that it was rather a missionary training school from which men and women could go out to teach ideals of Tuskegee to the rest of their race. He declared that the emphasis placed on the intellectual training is in keeping with the highest ideas of morality and industry, and that Tuskegee and its people send out their theories of industrial education.[30]

Jones not only talked about Booker T. Washington but also told the class that there were distinguished Negroes in various lines of work who were not as well known as Washington. "One of the highest expressions of Negro life, and achievement . . . was . . . [the work of] Dr. W. E. B. DuBois. . . . His great contention was that there was not so much a 'Negro Problem,' as Frederick Douglass once said, and that industrial education was no more a means for the complete development of the Negro than any other kind of education."[31] In addition, Jones read aloud passages from DuBois's book *Souls of Black Folk*.[32]

After preparing this seminar report, Jones became so excited about the idea of industrial education for blacks that he wrote a letter inquiring about summer school at Hampton Institute. Unfortunately the reply, dated May 9, 1907, stated that "on account of the Jamestown Exposition," the institute would not hold the usual summer session.[33]

Jones later said that his research project made him aware of the meaning of the poet's phrase "'Our echoes roll from soul to soul.'" He reflected that Mark Hopkins had taught Gen. Samuel Chapman Armstrong, that Armstrong had taught and inspired Booker T. Washington, and that Washington in turn had inspired him. Jones wrote, "There is no doubt in my mind that Piney Woods School is the result of this fervent enthusiasm and study."[34]

With the assistance of his scholarship and by working part time, Jones successfully completed the requirements for the bachelor's degree, which he received from the University of Iowa in the spring of 1907. His intense interest in Tuskegee and Hampton institutes continued, however, and he often considered himself to have been "in spirit a graduate of the two schools."[35]

Why did Jones, a Midwesterner, choose to come to Mississippi when he graduated from the University of Iowa? He received many job offers, including the principalship of a school in Missouri. His brilliancy would have assured him of a high place in the political councils of his race. Why did he pawn a graduation present from the fraternity to buy a ticket south? In view of Jones's first venture away from home, it is probable that he was—as he later said—heeding a partly unconscious urge, perhaps following a modern version of the adage "go West, young man." He was certainly also responding to Professor Holtzclaw's invitation, extended during a visit to Iowa, to come to Utica Institute.[36] As time passed Jones believed that he had received guidance. He wrote:

> I packed my trunk, and without notifying relatives or friends, I set out. I first went to Arkansas to become used to the Southern climate. Here I found a job looking after a horse and carriage and milking a cow. Meanwhile I was in correspondence with Dr. Booker T. Washington's great Tuskegee Institute and was in line for a place there, but decided to go to a little school in Hinds County, Mississippi, an outgrowth of Tuskegee.[37]

Before coming to Utica Institute as director of the academic program, he stopped at Tuskegee to visit his friend George Washington Carver, whom he had known in Iowa. Later, representing Utica Institute, Jones traveled throughout Mississippi and became acquainted with its people. His earlier background and these new experiences led him to think of starting his own school. Forten Weathersby, returning his son to Utica Institute, suggested the D'Lo community as a possible location, and Jones listened with interest.

A School Comes to Piney Woods 27

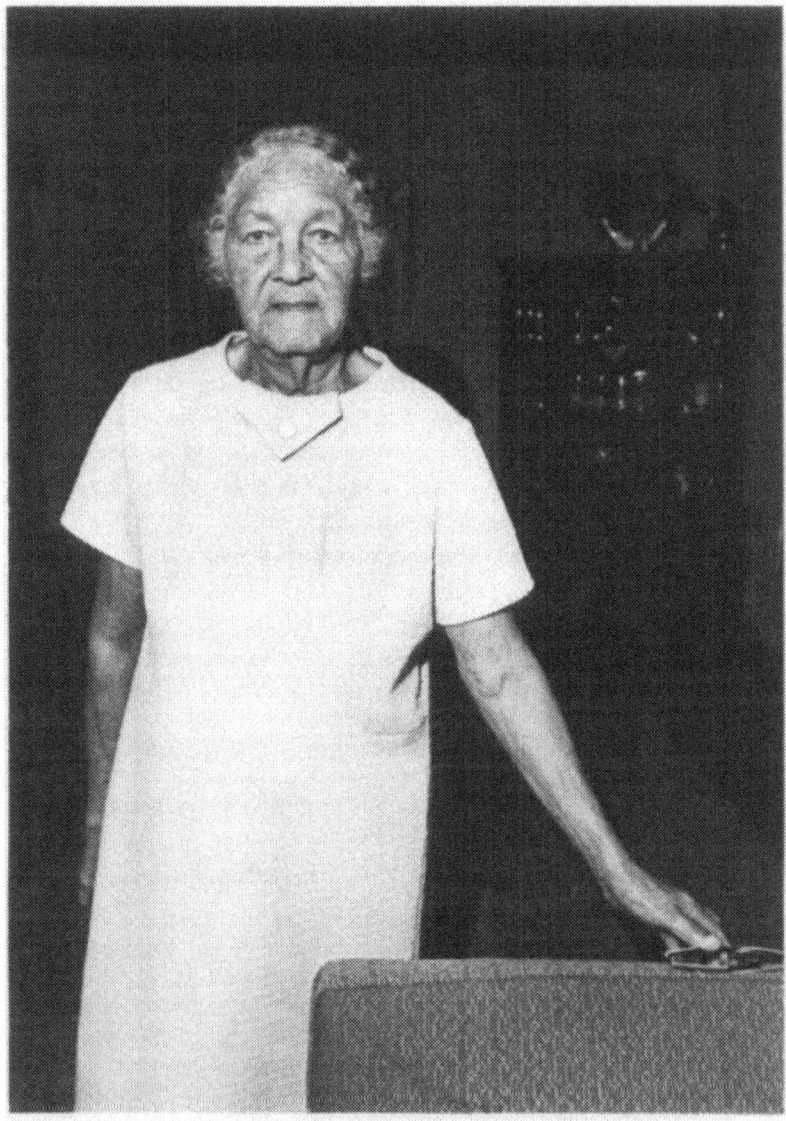

Eva Spell Weathersby (1893–) graduated from Piney Woods in 1918 in the first high school graduating class. (Photo courtesy of Roland Freeman)

Eva S. Weathersby recalled that her father-in-law, Forten Weathersby, had told Jones that the St. John's Church convention had raised money and had bought five acres of land for a D'Lo school. During the school's Christmas holiday of 1908, Jones visited the Weathersbys' home and the local community and participated in the festivities. Having observed living conditions in the area, Jones concluded, following his return to Utica Institute, that the people needed help in improving their means of basic survival. They needed to know how "to raise sufficient food to feed their families; how to perform more skilled jobs than chopping cotton." For the remainder of the term he sought to reeducate himself by reading and by studying farm problems discussed in pamphlets from the Iowa Corn Growers Association and from other groups and agencies. In 1909 he determined to leave his position at Utica, which he was said to have discharged with prudence and wisdom.[38]

Leola Hughes was seventeen when Jones came to Piney Woods.

> I remember the first time I saw [Dr. Jones]. He come in here a stranger and he was trying to get acquainted with all the neighbors. He really wanted a school. They wanted him to start one. He was clean faced and looked more like a boy than a man.
>
> He ate at my folks home and all over the community. People were nice to him. They tried to help him in every way they could. My mother even give him a couple of quilts. He really acted like he appreciated them being nice to him.[39]

Jones wrote about his activities during that first year.

> I saw that the future of the majority of the people must be as country-folk. . . . It was clear that the base of operation must be in the kitchen, the household, the garden, and the farm. So I talked diversified farming and around the firesides at night we figured out the cost of raising ten-cent cotton and buying fifteen-cent bacon, and ninety-cent corn from the meat-houses and corncribs of the North. I showed the folly of saving the worst land for the corn crop, from which they must derive their living, and of going to the crib in the spring and picking up anything left for seed corn, instead of selecting their seed in the field. . . . Meanwhile in the

homes I told the women about sanitary cooking and whitewash, and sometimes I applied the whitewash myself.

In this way I traveled all over Rankin County and a part of Simpson, sometimes astride a mule, sometimes in an ox-wagon, but more often afoot, sometimes walking eighteen or twenty miles a day.[40]

Jones attended and spoke at several of the annual church association meetings, and the concerns he expressed were not always greeted with understanding. He wrote: "Those who were at the head of affairs were as jealous of their positions as if they had been rulers of principalities. . . . They did not permit me to come before the body or take any part in the proceedings, and I found myself completely 'frozen out' on a sizzling August day."[41] On one occasion the congregation accused Forten Weathersby, the convention president, of having imported a "furriner," and the Dixon family, fearful of losing its influence in the community arranged for election of a new president.

Some time later Jones left the D'Lo area and went to Braxton to seek support for his school among the white townsfolk. He began by opening an account with one dollar at the Braxton Bank, where Mr. Wiley P. Mangum was the cashier. Hearing of Jones's plans for the school, Mangum was encouraging and offered to help as he could.

Jones next called on Mr. John Webster, the owner of a local sawmill. Webster was at first discouraging, expressing more interest in his sawmill than in "nigger education." As he spoke with Jones, however, he "remembered a vow he had made when he was a lad and had seen his grandfather mercilessly beat an adult Negro slave. His vow was to never forget the cruelty of the old man, to exercise kindness and mercy towards the Negro." Webster then promised not to stand in the way of the school; Jones should, however, see other people in the community and find out how they stand.[42]

Webster gave Jones a list of the community leaders whose approval would be needed. They included: Bob Hemphill, Anderson Pruitt, William Pattie, Gabe Jones, Eddie Ammons, and Roy Pattie, all of whom lived north of Piney Woods. In Braxton, Webster recommended that Jones talk with R. F. Everett and Wiley P. Mangum at the bank; J. P. Cox; the Barwick brothers; and Mrs. Caline Barwick.[43] Recalling these early days years later, Webster wrote:

> At that time, nearly every man in the country, including merchants and farmers, was getting . . . money out of the sawmill. Naturally, I would have some influence in the community. Besides, I wasn't one of "them furiners," some of whom were drifting in. I was a native product. I was employing both Negro and White labor on the same terms; most of them, boys I had been raised with. When Jones went out to interview these farmers round about, he would always say, "I have been talking to Mr. Webster and he said so far as he was concerned it was all right, so I have come to get your consent also.[44]

Jones immediately became the chief topic of conversation at the Comby Sawmill post office and store.

> "Well, what do you think of that nigger school?"
> "Well, I don't know. Did that nigger come to see you, too?"
> "Yes."
> "What do you think about it?"
> "Well, I think it's a good thing. He says he ain't gwine to teach 'em so much book larnin', but he wants to learn 'em to do more and better work, so when we wants good work done we can git it. That nigger seems like a good nigger. I like him."
> "Yes, and he said he wanted we white folks to be satisfied and willin' for him to have the school."[45]

Significantly, Webster observed: "This working or industrial agricultural school was the only kind that could have been established here at that time, for a book larnin' school for the Negroes would have gotten no local support whatever, and Jones would have aroused prejudices that would have been fatal, for a Negro wasn't supposed to read and write and especially how to figure. If his name was wanted for legal purposes, he made his cross mark (X)."[46]

Jones had arrived in Piney Woods in May 1909 with no funds

for his project, and September found him no better off financially. Though he had informed both the white and black communities of his plans, he had few resources with which to build a school.

He met his current expenses from the few cents that the people collected for him at their Sunday church meetings. By October 1909 he had aroused white and black interest, an achievement about which he was enthusiastic because long rains had produced one of the poorest crop seasons in the history of the county. No one had any money, and as was customary, the merchants had extended provisions and clothing to local blacks in the expectation of a better season next year.

There was still no sign of the support that Jones most wanted from the black community, however, and months of effort seemed to have yielded discouraging results. Then, one day as Jones sat on a log contemplating his failure, the situation changed. A boy accompanied Jones, and Jones offered the child something to read. The boy shook his head, saying, "I can't read.... I was bound out when a lad and never got to go to school and ain't been free long.'" Jones then began to teach him, remembering as he did so President Garfield's words that Mark Hopkins on one end of a log and a student on the other would constitute a university. It occurred to him, as he later wrote, that he, Jones,

> surely ought to be able to teach these illiterate boys and girls without the formality of buildings and desks and blackboards. So the inspiration came to me to open school under the old cedar tree, in God's out-of-doors, with His vast blue dome for our schoolhouse, and I set out to notify the farmers around that school would open on the next Monday morning at the cedar tree on the old Mordecai Harris place.... On Monday morning three boys met me and a few of the old brethren. We assembled under the tree on some pine logs, and after singing "Praise God from whom all blessings flow," reading lessons from the Bible, and offering prayer, declared school open.
>
> The next day I had a few more students, and the number grew until there were some twenty-nine. Each new addition meant more

This log sheep shed provided space for classrooms and living quarters for the Jones family and school staff when the school first opened. This log cabin has been enclosed in a cement block structure for its preservation.

> pine logs for seats. After a few weeks two of the students, a young man and a young woman who I had taught before coming to Piney Woods, joined me, and several more insisted upon coming though I had no place for them to stay. The young man was a very good carpenter and the young woman fairly well advanced in her studies. They became my efficient assistants.[47]

Jones's two helpers were William F. Yancy and Docia Weathersby. Yancy had learned carpentry from his father and grandfather. Leola Hughes was in the first class, with Docia and Lessie Weathersby, Mary Weathersby, and Lottie Gray. The boys included Bill Dixon and Jack and Early Weathersby.

In the chilly days of November, the students built fires to keep warm during classes. Soon, however, Jones began to think of moving the school into a tumbledown cabin nearby. After making inquiries he learned that it belonged to a former slave named Edward Nelson Taylor. Jones had met this man earlier and had borrowed $125 from him without interest or security to pay a local family for the death of a horse that Jones had ridden.[48] This earlier contact encouraged Jones to believe that Tay-

Edward Nelson Taylor (far left) was an ex-slave who gave the forty acres on which Laurence Jones started Piney Woods Country Life School. Taylor is pictured here with Jones (center) and L. G. Wells, Jones's instructor at the University of Iowa.

lor would help him, although the former slave had a reputation for being stingy and for foreclosing on loans to blacks. In addition, Taylor's background suggested that he might be personally sympathetic to Jones's cause.

After the Civil War Taylor had gone to Rockford, Illinois, and had attended school for three terms near Cherry Valley. He had subsequently moved to Keokuk, Iowa, where he worked as a barber with an old Frenchman. Upon returning to Mississippi he was able to buy several hundred acres of land and to save some money.[49]

On the day that Jones went to inquire about the cabin, he had to wait until Taylor had finished plowing in the field. The two men then ate supper and talked until three o'clock the next morning. During that time Taylor "decided to give forty acres of land and fifty dollars in money toward the substantial beginning of the school. The next day we went down and looked over the forty acres, and the following Saturday he went to town and deeded the property to the trustees of the Piney Woods Industrial School and gave a check for fifty dollars."[50] The quick execution of this transaction demonstrated Taylor's businesslike character, upon which Jones learned to rely.

Though Jones and Taylor were excited at the prospect of building the school, when they announced the gift at the local church, they were surprised to hear one of the deacons say: "'I ain't goin' to have nothin' to do with it. If Ed Taylor gave you dat land and money there's a trick to it somewheres. Taylor ain't done dat if there ain't a trick to it." The meeting became more enthusiastic, however, when Taylor and Jones declared that they would build the school even if they had to do it alone.[51]

In spite of such initial expressions of distrust, the friendship between the two men grew. In those early days Taylor often traveled with Jones. A member of a Tougaloo College audience recalled their visits there on several occasions. After Jones had described his struggles to win white and colored support for his school, he usually mentioned Taylor's gifts, saying, "I want you to see the man who made it all possible for me to establish Piney Woods School." When the applause began to diminish, Taylor, bowing awkwardly, would say, "Ladies and gentlemen, all Fesser Jones said 'bout me is nothing but the truth."[52] Taylor was a true friend to Jones as long as he lived.

Jones had now gained the support of one man, but he did not cease trying to enlist the help of the entire black community. While riding through the settlements he secured some small pledges, the largest being fifteen dollars from Rev. Hector McLaurin, one of the most prosperous black farmers in the area. Amon Gibson, another farmer, volunteered to haul the first load of lumber to make benches and bookshelves in the log cabin. Others said that they would help "rive out de bods." In this community spirit, the log cabin was whitewashed and furnished. One end became living quarters for Jones and Yancy. The other end became a schoolhouse, with a chapel, study hall, recitation room, office, sewing room, and carpenter's and basket-making shops.

Jones then learned that the community was "due a little schooling from the county." A one-room school had been set aside for blacks living in Simpson and Rankin counties, and its teacher was supposed to receive a salary of fifteen to eighteen dollars a month for a three- or four-month school term. This school seemed to have little future, and Jones was therefore permitted to incorporate it into his own plans.[53] Ralph Maddox, superintendent of schools in Simpson County, "encouraged the Rankin County superintendent, 'Mot' Myers, to support Jones by giving Piney Woods the monthly appropriation that had . . . gone to the little one-teacher school." Maddox also assisted Jones by helping him arrange for teachers certified to teach at Piney Woods.[54]

During these days Webster remained the school's most important white ally. When Jones went to the Comby post office, he consulted with Webster, who made his office typewriter available at noon and in the evenings, so that Jones could write letters to prospective donors in Iowa. Jones had assured Webster and the black and white communities that his objectives were to teach trades, farming, cooking, sewing, better work habits, and the care of animals and equipment. Webster once asked, "You think you can make better workers out of the niggers?" Jones replied, "That is what I hope to do. To make better farmers, teach them how to be more saving, and eventually to bring them a higher standard of living." Webster promised to give Jones the first 10,000 feet of lumber and credit to buy all that was needed for the proposed building.[55]

Thus encouraged, during the spring of 1910 Jones scheduled a "great meeting of the people" to discuss the proposed construction. He later recalled that "some eleven hundred came afoot, on horseback, on ox-wagons and vehicles of every description." R. F. Everett, president of the Braxton Bank, John Webster, and approximately twenty-three other Braxton whites were present. The local blacks included Amon Gibson, Edward Nelson Taylor, Georgia Byrd, and Hector McLaurin. After making a speech, Jones passed the hat. The response was again encouraging, the donations including food, labor, and building materials as well as small amounts of cash.[56]

The community folk helped erect the first permanent building as they had helped repair the old cabin. After they had finished the foundation and the framing and had put on the weather boarding, however, a gulf storm almost completely destroyed their work. Disheartened but still determined, Jones and the community folk, including some women, "borrowed some jacks from the mills and railroad company and set to work to put the whole back in shape."[57] The finished structure was named Taylor Hall.

In building Taylor Hall, Jones instituted the custom of calling on the community folk for "work days." On such occasions members of the Mothers' Club cooked "som'in to eat" and brought it to the school. Nellie Flowers Cox, a former president of the club, recalled that Steven Cox (her husband), Amon Gibson, Hector McLaurin, and Elijah Campbell had helped Jones on work days. Most of these men had children or grandchildren in Piney Woods School.[58]

The new building housed approximately eighty-five students, who ranged in ages from six to sixty. Their 1909–1910 curriculum included English, sewing, basketry, broom making, woodwork, and beginning flower gardening. The Piney Woods students found themselves able to relate these subjects with little difficulty. The "closing exercises consisted of essays on housekeeping, cooking, sewing, gardening and manual training."[59] They inspired the students to apply what they had learned at Piney Woods when they went home.

During that first summer, Jones and many of the students worked at the school, "trying to make a little crop" without any animals to help them till the land. They also continued soliciting funds by mail. Although they sent out a thousand letters, however, they received only one response. Remembering his uncle, Prior Foster, Jones decided to travel to Iowa in pursuit of funds. Jones did not raise large sums of money on this trip, but he learned how to present his project to the public and he gained some friends outside Piney Woods.

In the fall of 1910, Piney Woods School opened with five

teachers including William F. Yancy and his bride, Mary Martin, former student of Jones's. Miss Docia Weathersby returned as a teacher, and Louis Watson, a young high school graduate whom Jones had met during the summer, volunteered his services. Watson had been working in Des Moines, Iowa, as a porter. Watson and the other teachers dedicated themselves to teaching approximately one hundred students without pay.

Watson taught academic subjects all day and at night often worked as the bookkeeper and registrar, keeping records of money spent and received and of the work time and grades of the students. When Christmas came, his mother sent candles and decorations from which Watson made Christmas boxes using pasteboard and tissue paper. He also painted motto cards for each of the students and for many of their parents. During that winter Watson became severely ill from exhaustion and from inadequate diet, medical care, and housing, and he died two weeks after Christmas. Thanks to his efforts, however, for the first time many of the students and the community folks celebrated Christmas with "a sermon in the afternoon, a sacred concert at night and a Christmas tree gaily decorated and brilliant with dozens of candles. . . ." In contrast to earlier times, "not a gun was fired, not an unpleasant incident marred the blessed holiday. . . . The eyes of the little boys and girls sparkled as they feasted upon the tree and as the names of the different ones were called for the boxes of nuts and candy."[60]

During this second year Taylor learned of a piano that could be purchased for thirty dollars. To pay for it Amon Gibson sold his last bale of hay and donated the instrument to the school. During this second year, too, the school established its practice of asking students to work half of each day and to attend school the other half. It was also decided that school would close during the first week of May.

Awards were made to show community folk the students' newly acquired skills. Mr. W. P. Mangum gave a gold medal to the girl who had made the greatest progress in cooking, as demonstrated by the preparation and serving of a meal before the audience. Another girl cut out and made a dress. Some students set type and printed instructions for farmers, and one young man exhibited a good razorback pig that he had raised.

The school, having paid no salaries, closed debt-free. During the summer of 1911 its staff and students prepared for the next school term by cultivating food, assisted the community, and solicited funds. Two of the teachers helped students tend a small farm and garden. During this second year they "were able to purchase a 'donkey' for twenty dollars . . ., enabling them to make a small crop."[61] A third teacher went "back in the forest among the people organizing rural school improvement associations, cooking classes, corn clubs and poultry clubs."[62] Jones himself returned to Iowa to launch a fund-raising campaign.

Beyond the immediate bounds of the school and school-sponsored programs, most of the workers found abundant opportunity for service in the community. They helped residents write letters to (and read letters from) sons who had left the area in search of work; explained passages of Scripture; helped settle family and neighborhood quarrels, through arbitrating on occasion; and sometimes copied documents for white people who lived nearby.

As it had the year before, on the third Monday in October 1911 the school opened with five teachers under thirty years old. On that first day each person told how he or she had applied some skill acquired at Piney Woods on the farm or in the home or community. During the year 1911–1912 the school received a bigger printing press and a typewriter. The closing exercises in May 1912 and the summer work followed the tradition established during the previous two years. The donkey acquired the year before was supplemented by a strong horse, which made farming easier that summer.

Jones later fondly recalled the school's first students, "big gawky country boys and girls who came with their earthly possessions in a sack"—and sometimes with no sack at all. Their education consisted

> far more . . . in doing than in books. It was they who would voluntarily disband classes to put the washing out or to get the fall

crop in. What they lacked in knowledge they made up in spirit and hard work. . . . They worked early and late, and studied if there was any time left over. . . . Those pioneers of the laundry and kitchen and clearing gangs . . . worked through unbelievably long hours. . . . They sat on crude benches that had never known a planer's knife. . . . [They sang] hymns to the tune of a piano that had cost thirty dollars; and they did not despise the light of a pine knot if the kerosene gave out.[63]

The community was plainly benefiting from Piney Woods School.

2

Education for the Folks

Piney Woods School was conceived during an era when dynamic forces were being harnessed to develop the rural South. Its financial support was both private and public. In 1862 the Morrill Land Grant Act provided funds for an agricultural and mechanical arts college in each state. In 1871 Alcorn became the first land grant college for blacks. Apart from the 1890 Land Grant Act, little other federal support was legislated until 1906, when federal farm agents were placed in Texas, ushering in an era of farm demonstration work by home and farm agents in the communities of rural America.

In 1907 the Anna T. Jeanes Fund was established for use "solely towards the maintenance and assistance of rural, community and country schools for Southern Negroes and *not for use or benefit at large institutions*, but for the purpose of rudimentary education."[1] It inspired teachers to draw on resources of the community and to coordinate their efforts to acquire needed services. Utica, Prentiss, and Piney Woods were private schools of Mississippi that made the intended use of the fund in their regions.

Jones professed to have had the first Jeanes teacher in Mississippi as one of his students at Piney Woods.

When the lady in Philadelphia, Miss Anna T. Jeanes, first left that money [$1,000,000 in 1907] to supply Jeanes teachers in the South, I thought it was a mighty good thing and I got interested in it. There was a professor down at Tulane University who was interested and we started corresponding about it. He invited me down and I went down and visited with him at Tulane. We decided we'd make a beginning. We had a lady, Miss Mary E. Martin, here at Piney Woods School, who was a very fine student. She had some age on her and was more reliable and trustworthy than a small caliber student and in fact she was recognized by the students and always called Miss Martin. So I introduced her to the man from Tulane University when he came here. We decided we'd start out with Miss Martin and she was the first one that did any Jeanes work in the state of Mississippi.[2]

Although Miss Martin was possibly one of the first eighteen to twenty-six Jeanes teachers in the state,[3] sources disagree as to who was first. Mary Martin did work with Jones in Simpson County from 1910 to 1912. She was paid through Simpson County and was directly responsible to county officials, but she used Piney Woods School as her base. She visited homes and assisted women and girls in canning, poultry raising, homemaking, and child rearing. Later Jeanes teachers were usually not stationed at Piney Woods. When Piney Woods graduates such as Ernestine Pippins Carter of Rankin County and Bettye Mae Jack of Scott County became Jeanes teachers, however, they maintained a close working relationship with Piney Woods.[4]

In 1911 the county training school program began with support from the John F. Slater Fund. The program required cooperation with local agencies that agreed to share the initial expenditure and promised continued support. The Slater Fund thus encouraged the establishment of public high schools for blacks and a large consolidation movement that involved combining the rural elementary schools in areas densely populated by Negroes. This movement supplemented the efforts of Piney Woods in a broader community.

As early as 1911 Piney Woods School's educational program

benefited the community almost as much as its students. Its extension work consisted of programs of self-help such as farmers' conferences. (A Rural School Improvement Association was also planned but did not come into being. It was intended to assist more than five thousand people indirectly,[5] and Jones may have envisioned it as a link between Piney Woods and other rural schools. Despite the failure of RSIA, however, the farm agents, Jeanes teachers, and the consolidation movement gradually began to spur development in the area.)

Though Piney Woods had had farmers' conferences from its inception, the conference of November 1911 marked the first visit of a Union captain, Asa Turner, a remarkable white farmer from Iowa who had been a Confederate prisoner in Mississippi.[6] Turner spoke at another conference in January 1912, and hundreds reportedly attended to hear his words. Turner also lectured at the white Braxton high school and at the Simpson County agricultural meeting in Mendenhall, supplementing agricultural advice with stories of his experiences on the Iowa prairie.[7]

Captain Turner experienced life at Piney Woods when he came to speak. The March 1912 *Pine Torch* reported, "We gave Cap't Turner an opportunity of realizing our pioneer life by assigning him to a night in the log cabin in which we [stayed]. . . . It has a large fireplace, which we ourselves built in the frontier style, mud and sticks, which we heaped high with blazing pine knots and showed him how to roast sweet potatoes and gubers in the ashes."[8] Before he retired, Captain Turner participated in Principal Jones's evening devotion in the soft glow of the firelight. Such sharing at Piney Woods was the seed from which Piney Woods community relationships continued to grow.

Community meetings were often called in the school chapel. For example, in 1912 the county supervisor for the white neighbors at Comby called two meetings at Piney Woods to discuss the location of dipping vats for the eradication of cattle ticks.[9] As the years passed, Piney Woods found itself serving a community increasingly aware of participating in national trends. For example, passage of the Smith-Lever Act, on May 8, 1914, encouraged an agricultural extension system similar to that sponsored by the Slater Fund but depending specifically on cooperation between the U.S. Department of Agriculture and the land grant colleges. Federal grants-in-aid for extension programs were to be matched by state appropriations. In general, the Smith-Lever Act sought to disseminate improved farming methods and to raise the standard of living for farmers. Its direct instrument was the county farm agent, who visited farmers throughout the county.

Piney Woods almost naturally evolved in accordance with the recommendations of the committee of the General Education Board Conference on Negro Education, held on July 8–10, 1915. It advocated partial support for programs of education for boys and girls within the classroom and much more support for "the education of all the people in the locality in which the school is placed so that ultimately the people of the locality, with possibly a few friends outside, will care for the school."[10] The Smith-Hughes Act of 1917 was a broadening of the Smith-Lever Act to promote instruction in agriculture and the trades through a federal board for vocational education.

The conferences and curriculum at Piney Woods not only exemplified but advanced the trends of the times. The Piney Woods program was certainly similar to the curriculum of the training schools being established with Slater Fund support and also resembled the plans followed by many Smith-Hughes teachers. The schools were community centered, aiming to improve the living conditions within a society that remained rigidly segregated (schools often sought the permission of landlords to involve their tenants). Influential whites cooperated, aware that their own interests could be served by making the Negroes economically more useful.

During the early days Piney Woods certainly had good relations with influential whites. In addition to its success in eliciting white cooperation and support, Piney Woods students were allowed to participate in white fairs. The February 1917 *Pine Torch* reported that the school's exhibit at one fair was visited by the wife of state senator Theodore G. Bilbo for about an hour. The exhibit won the largest number of prizes in the "special" category.[11] The information disseminated at the farmers' conference had made success possible.

The conference of February 1917 was the largest ever held at Piney Woods School. More than 500 farmers, including some whites, were present to hear R. S. Wilson of the U.S. Department of Agriculture. When it came Jones's turn to speak, he talked about the large number of blacks leaving the state in search of work in cities, such as Chicago, where industry was prospering with the increased demand of wartime. Jones asked the farmers to stay and help develop Mississippi, and he urged blacks not to join the exodus to the North. For the betterment of their race they should concentrate their efforts at home in the South, even though after graduation every door upward was closed. "Not a business house, not a bank, not a railroad gives us the right to make good. As I see it, we are a child race that we have been free for only fifty years."[12]

By 1919 more than six hundred earnest farmers from two states and nineteen settlements had participated in the conferences, and "more than six thousand acres of land had been purchased by colored farmers in the vicinity of the school . . . more than was purchased in the previous twenty years." Speakers such as Captain Turner and Prof. P. G. Holden sought to inspire the farmers "to better living as well as better systems of working their land."[13] By these means and others Piney Woods exerted a great impact upon the community.

From its inception Piney Woods had sent its teachers to "do extension work . . . , sometimes in a single home, again in a neighborhood meeting or in a country church, sometimes simply in an outdoor meeting called for the formation of an improvement club."[14] The "long extension trips into the backwoods over rough roads and dim trails" carried modern farm life practices to the most remote Negro families.[15] Such trips also enabled former students to apply what they had learned.

Dignitaries in the foreground are (from left) R. F. Everett, President of the Braxton Bank; Asa Turner of Iowa; Laurence Jones; J. P. Cox, Vice-President of the Braxton Bank; P. G. Holden, Iowa State College professor; and Wiley P. Mangum, cashier of Braxton Bank. In the foreground are students in uniform, the dress required for students for many years to minimize distinctions between the rich and poor students.

As the impact of the Smith-Lever Act reached the Mississippi black folk, however, it was no longer necessary for Piney Woods to send its faculty to do extension work. Home demonstration agents came to the area, and some used Piney Woods as a base. They worked in the field every day, entering into the life of a farmer and inspiring him and his wife to better and more intelligent cultivation practices. Gertrude Carter, the first Negro home demonstration agent for Rankin County, was a Piney Woods graduate. She was employed as county home economist by the Agricultural Extension Service of Mississippi State College but had no office there in the early days.[16]

A 1927 Piney Woods graduate, Robert E. Lee, began working with the U.S. Department of Agriculture to help the farmers of the area. His job included counseling the six thousand white and colored farmers on soil erosion, stock raising, and improved farming practices. He was also charged with executive and practical management of the 4-H Clubs of Rankin County, which had 450 members.[17] By arrangement with the home economist, Piney Woods School was used during the summer months as a camp for Negro boys and girls.[18] "More than 150 4-H boys and their sponsors and the County Agents, from 30 counties held a three-day roundup at Piney Woods the last week in June" 1949.[19]

More important than the farm agents and the home demonstration agents for Piney Woods School's relationship with the larger community was the government representative assigned to the area under the terms of the Smith-Hughes Act. J. D. Hardy worked part time at Piney Woods for the development of agriculture and part time in the community. During the 1924–1925 school year his salary was paid partly by the U.S. Department of Agriculture and partly by Piney Woods School. Hardy conducted conferences, clubs, and projects that involved the men and boys of Rankin County. He also provided information on planting, prices, and the preparation of certain reports. Often he even sold the farmers' crops and even wrote letters for them.[20] A typical year-end report by Hardy follows.

1. Met with people at various centers and explained how he could help them
2. Conducted a community survey
3. Assigned 20 projects to boys—corn, cotton, cucumbers, hogs. . . .
4. Basic achievements
    a. Visited 127 projects
    b. Repaired cotton planter valued at $2.00

c. Terraced land for four farmers to 60 acres of land valued at $100.00
d. Made self-feeders for one flock of chickens valued at $7.50
e. Vaccinated 59 cows, horses and goats at $.60 each ($35.40)
f. Culled three flocks of poultry, $6.00
g. Vaccinated 80 hogs for cholera at $.60 each, $48.00
h. Treated 20 hogs for the cholera $.40, $8.00
i. Community Fair with more than 500 people present including 100 or more white people and about 35 automobiles on the ground worth $300.00 to the community
j. Pooled a car of fertilizer at Belpine, saving the people $50.00
k. Boys were given instruction along their prospective lines of project work during the regular school term and farmers were being instructed during the evenings

Total value of community work during the year was $556.90 plus $1,571.80 total profit from the project work, making a grand total of $2,128.79.[21]

A native of Newton, in Newton County, Mississippi, Hardy understood the needs of the community and worked well with its people. He arrived in Piney Woods about 1922, and shortly thereafter he married Jones's sister, Nellie. Area residents recall Hardy's work in Piney Woods especially vividly in connection with the community fairs from about 1925 to 1932. Lenzie Braddy, one of Hardy's former students, described these events.

> The fairs we had at Piney Woods School would take the whole communities of Rankin and Simpson counties. Professor Hardy would be somewhere in the community every day and see what the folks were doing with their gardens, because he would always be trying to work up a community fair—but it helped Piney Woods School, too. He was teaching agriculture for Piney Woods, but he would get out in the community to work up the fair, traveling many miles. The fair would be two to three days, and people would look forward to it. Prof. Hardy would take his boys out, dig up collards, flowers, corn, cane, and pull pigs in for exhibit for those that couldn't get them there for the community stand. After I had graduated and married I used my truck to pick up stuff for

Lenzie Braddy is today a proud service station-grocery store and trailer park owner on Highway 49 near Braxton. He graduated from Piney Woods in the 1930s and has sent all his children to school there. (Photo courtesy of Roland Freeman)

folks who didn't have a way to deliver it up there. Prof. Hardy's agriculture class would go over to the dairy barn and get one or two fine Holsteins. See, at that time they had Holstein instead of Ayrshire cows. . . . We'd bring some of the finest hogs over. Mr. Green Hicks would bring a horse out there, and the boys that he'd be training, he would let them shoe one.

Agricultural teachers and agents like Mr. R. E. Lee of Brandon would be there. The campus would be filled from almost one entrance to the other. People would come from the schools by the school bus loads, get them a parking place, put up their displays, go to dinner in the dining hall, and come back to the activities and have much fun.

They would have a greasy pole with a ten-pound ham on top. We would slip and climb and slip and climb until we got the ham. They would have a sack race. They'd have a guinea race. You could get in a sack and try to catch the guinea, or you could get on your feet and try to catch the guinea.

We had us a music machine up there playing. Prof. Hardy had me over it. In other words, Prof. Lee from Oakley—Neal and Oakley Cafe—let us have a machine. They just played their records and had fun. That's really what it was for. He said he wanted one time of the year for the community to enjoy themselves at Piney Woods.

We would have a concert that night and a judging contest. At every night activity Mr. Jones would make a short speech of welcome. He'd say, "This really ain't my school. It's you-all's. Anybody that wants to come here, if you haven't got a penny, I'll never turn you down."

Then we would have some kind of religious service after it was all over with. All that's a certain outlook folks enjoyed. They got to enjoy their work. I never know'd them to fight or anything. They didn't have no police other than the night watchman.[22]

From their beginning in the mid-1920s, the fairs grew in size and quality each year. Meeting in December 1933 the Piney Woods Fair Association planned its first countywide fair, which would last for two days, October 12 and 13, 1934. With Hardy serving as secretary and with R. E. Lee and Gertrude Carter as assistants, the Fair Association planned activities more ambitious than ever before. It invited quartets, choirs, and other musical groups. It scheduled two nights of movies obtained from the state Board of Development at Jackson and from International Harvester Company of Chicago. The planned sports and games included round robin baseball, sack races, dodge ball, and pop the whip.[23]

The printed program for that year announced the "Community Fair at Piney Woods" for October 13 and 14. Joe E. Byrd was then president of the Fair Association. Cash prizes for items entered into the various categories ranged from $5.00 to $0.25. The various categories or departments included horse and mule, cattle, swine, field crops, Smith-Hughes boys' section, garden, women's and girls' sewing, canning, culinary, and poultry. In addition, there was a free-for-all department that awarded prizes to the school with the greatest number of children present, to the biggest family, to heaviest, tallest, and shortest persons, and to the best liar.

These fairs captured the hearts and imagination of the people perhaps more than any other activity at Piney Woods. Through them and their promoter, the school further deepened its relationship with the community. By means of programs such as the farmers' conferences and the fairs, Piney Woods made a unique contribution to the development of the rural blacks in the area. "Through the extension work of the school—reaching 15,000 Negroes annually—and the influence of its graduates, three-fourths of the colored farmers in Rankin and Simpson Counties, adjacent to the school, own land, as against less than 5 percent when Piney Woods was started."[24]

The general theories propounded by educators concerned with the American rural population in the 1930s often reflected successful practice in schools like Piney Woods. For example, Mabel Carney, head of the department for rural education of Columbia University, concluded after visiting Piney Woods and several community homes "that Piney Woods was serving a far greater body of people than the few hundred on the campus." In the 1920s and 1930s she advocated the development of rural education programs like those under way at Piney Woods.[25] Leo M. Favrot in 1936 espoused ideals that Piney Woods School had pursued from its earliest days. He said: "Education will have far more effect if the school can assume the role of a lighthouse and serve both to illumine and to guide the path of the rural dweller . . . , aid it in developing a better sense of values of the worthwhile things in life."[26]

Piney Woods thus became a beacon not only to farmers but to other groups as well. Jones saw that the school's activities extended beyond the local and state communities to the nation. He described his decision to support the First World War on the home front:

> To us in Piney Woods the World War brought new responsibilities and obligations just as it did to everyone else. At the very beginning there loomed before me the Officers' Training Camp at Des Moines, to which many of my friends were going. This meant getting into the game early and greater honor; on the other hand there was the family—my wife, mother, two little boys—and then there was the school. Meanwhile I was under a Chautauqua contract to visit some eighty old towns, and I was also under contract with the State Department of Education for my second term as director of a summer normal school for some three hundred Negro

teachers. I turned to my wife and dearest friends for advice, and their conviction was that I should follow out the duties nearest me. When I came to the county seat in the second registration, moreover, and fulfilled the requirements of the Government, my name was officially placed in Class 4A. It was galling to me to think that I was Class 4, when I had determined that in everything I should be in Class 1; but I resolved that if I could not be in Class 1 on the firing line in France, I would be in class 1 on the firing line in America, and so I plunged into war work, and in every address I delivered that summer, I put every ounce of energy and enthusiasm.[27]

In his chosen state of Mississippi, Jones served as state and county speaker for five Liberty Loan campaigns; as chairman of the Colored Red Cross workers in two counties, himself conducting two drives; as a speaker during the Thrift Stamp campaigns; and as the only member of his race to hold an executive office in the first United War Fund drive (he assisted J. C. Wilson, the executive director appointed to work with colored people).[28] As usual, Jones was an effective leader; in one county (Chickasaw) blacks actually oversubscribed their quota in the drive. Piney Woods was thus as active during the war as in the years before and after. After the armistice, when the veterans returned to their homes, the school joined the community in welcoming them back, offering the latest farm information through its extension programs.

Just as the leadership of Piney Woods had joined the community in supporting the war effort, it involved itself with the people during the Depression. At Piney Woods, as at many other educational institutions, funds were sometimes insufficient to meet the meager payroll. Still, although Piney Woods received fewer donations during the depression years, the school suffered relatively fewer hardships than more prosperous institutions. There were only two years, 1934 and 1935, when Piney Woods opened its doors late from lack of funds.[29] The school depended chiefly upon farm produce in an already poverty-stricken area, and it worked hard and struggled through hard times, supporting and benefiting from its neighbors as it always had.

Predictably, Piney Woods cooperated with the federal government's program for national uplift and recovery. The school's facilities were used for the Neighborhood Youth Administration (NYA), under the supervision of Olivia H. Smith of Jackson. NYA students were trained for domestic service in a new laundry and practice kitchen erected for the purpose. Many of the students came from Tougaloo, Jackson, and Rust colleges in Mississippi and from Straight and Southern universities in Louisiana. Others arrived from Biloxi, McComb, Handsboro, Magnolia, Gulfport, Canton, Brookhaven, Doddsville, and Jackson.

The community continued to profit from new programs and activities offered at Piney Woods, and it reaped new benefits from the school's growing success. Though Piney Woods depended less and less for its progress upon the freely given labor of community members, it continued to share with them. In addition to the farmers' conferences and the community fairs, community folk came to Piney Woods for programs on special occasions such as Thanksgiving and Christmas.

On Thanksgiving in 1921 Rev. Chester A. Greer, pastor of the Farish Street Baptist Church of Jackson, gave the message. It was followed by "an old-fashioned 'speaking' after the manner of our people." E. N. Taylor recounted how neighbors had come from miles around to clear land and prepare the cottage that first housed classes. Then Forten Weathersby told how he had come to the area and how he had struggled to help create a decent country school. Often after such "old-fashioned speaking" the students discovered a new reason for giving thanks.[30]

Perhaps the most important celebration that Piney Woods shared with the community occurred at Christmas. This had been an important holiday at the school since its second year of operation, when Louis Watson had worked so hard to recreate his Iowan Christmas. Nellie Cox and her daughter, Rose Brooks, recalled the Christmas bundles of clothing.

> People up north would send barrels and barrels of clothing, shoes and apples. They had a place down there that they'd put this stuff in [the Lunky]. My mother, Mrs. Singleton, and Mrs. Jones would

Every year packages arrived from the North in time to make Christmas bundles for the students and community people.

> open them barrels and boxes and classify out the stuff, like I do now. They'd fill a paper bag full of apples and oranges. Well, sometimes they'd have candy, you know. Mrs. Jones would get that and put it in there. They'd make everybody in the community a bundle of clothing, shoes, and things—whatever the families could use.[31]

At Christmas the school sent donors throughout the state and the nation holiday greetings in the form of holly and mistletoe, wreaths of pine cones and straw, and handmade hats and bags. In the early days students often worked all night making baskets and other Christmas gifts.[32]

Community folk and white neighbors in Braxton recalled being awakened on Christmas morning by the Piney Woods carolers. The 1949 *Pine Torch* said:

> An enjoyable feature of the Season is our Carolling groups, who sing for our neighbors about 4 o'clock Christmas morning. Two groups and their chaperones go out in opposite directions, sometimes going four or five miles. . . . When such carols as "Go Tell It On the Mountains," "Joy To The World," "Noel," "Away in a

Manger," "It Came Upon a Midnight Clear," "Hark, the Herald Angels Sing," "Silent Night! Holy Night!" etc. are sung by our students, the friends aroused from their peaceful sleep, come out and express the joy that they received from the songs which tell of the Saviour's birth. Many of the listeners bring out cake, fruit, nuts and candy as a mark of appreciation. Needless to say, the children go away pleased. When the singers return, they complete their journey with the singing of carols for each dormitory, the teachers' cottages and the President's home.[33]

In addition to visiting the homes, a caroling group always went to the Mississippi State Tuberculosis Sanitorium, especially to the colored infirmary. These small ways of sharing the spirit of Christmas made Piney Woods dear to the local residents and broadened the school's essential role as a center of cultural and educational opportunity.

Such positive community spirit enabled the school to combat not only obsolete farm methods but some superstitions as well.

Among the people who lived in the Piney Woods area in about 1922, Jones said, the "conjure man" and the "hoodoo woman" were still to be reckoned with. Jones mentioned local superstitions often. He recalled that once, when he had installed a skylight in a building, the local people had said that he did so in order to be closer to God. They also regarded his founding of the school as somehow placing him in closer touch with the Supreme Being or as evidence that Jones possessed some extraordinary power. On one occasion a man came asking for help in finding his wife, who had gone to a missionary meeting in the afternoon and had not returned home. The man worried that she had

> been runned off by some dev'lish conjure business. I's been livin' wid her nigh thirty years an' if you ain't never had nary one to do dat way, you doesn't know.... She' a good 'oman; it ain't none o' her doin's at all. It's dis way; an old widow 'oman lived on de place where we is, an' she moved away an' we 'greed to work de place dis year, an' den she'd 'cided to come back, an' case de man what ons de place refuse to knock out our 'greement, she's mad an' now she's gone an' put a spell on Hattie. Poor Hattie! She jes' don't know whar she is or what she's doin'. Fesser, plenty o' people don' belieb it, but dere's gophers an conjurers in New O'leans ain't neber been

here an' could tell you all you got here, an' dey could tear all your mind up in less 'an a week. De low-down rascals, dey ought to be hung. Some o' Virginny; it' called a jack; an' de debils can go to your house while you an' you' wife is sleepin' an' sprinkle some powder on de door step, er plant something dere, an' de nex' mornin' you steps over it an' dey's jest as good as got you as a dollar—

No, sir, I ain't hungry a bit; couldn't eat if I had to. I jes' got to keep walkin'. But you can help me, Fesser, You's got de sense; you can work it so dat she'll come back and never leave.[34]

Jones persuaded him to rest. When he woke up, the man felt sure that his Hattie had returned. "I knowed you could make your han' work if you would. . . . I's goin' home an' I knows I'll fin' Hattie dere." That Christmas he thanked Jones with a present of "a choice offering from a hog-killing" and said when he got home that day Hattie was there "an' mad as a wet hen, 'case I been out to hunt for her. . . . Don' you tell her nothin' 'bout my gettin' you ter use yo' han', Fesser, case she'd be madder 'n ever."[35]

The November 1932 *Pine Torch* listed various superstitions of Southerners.

To leave a chair rocking after you have been sitting in it is a sure sign that you will die soon.
Dropping a dish rag is a sure sign someone is coming hungry.
It's a sure sign of death if a bird flies into a house.
If a rooster crows in front of the door, it is a sure sign that someone is coming.[36]

Piney Woods School sought to substitute religious faith for local superstition. As in other areas, Jones influenced community values and mores not by lecturing the people but by setting an example and by involving parents and children alike in social and cultural activities. In this he was greatly assisted by his wife.

Jones first met Grace M. Allen during his junior year in college when they were both speaking at an Iowa City church. They maintained contact with each other, mainly through correspondence, and on June 29, 1912, they were married in Iowa City.

Principal Laurence Jones, his wife Grace, and their son Turner

Piney Woods Country Life School
Viewed Through the Camera Lens
of Roland Freeman
October 21, 1978

Piney Woods entrance

Campus scene

Math lesson

Elementary group instruction

High school English class

Elementary classroom

Piney Woods motto

The Office

Dry cleaning department

The school store

Farm maintenance

Data processing

Garden at "Little Boys" dorm

Intramural sports

Bible study

Administrative Staff, 1979 *(from left)* Vera Thomas, Coordinator of Administration and Records; Marvel Turner, Vice-President for Business Affairs; John Bernard Jones, Vice-President for Development; W. K. Jones, volunteer administrator in Academic Program; James S. Wade, President; John Haien, Jr., Vice-President for Buildings and Grounds; Mary Tyson, Art Instructor; Dr. Samuel McGee, Vice-President of Academic Affairs.

Dulany Hall patio

Site of the first Piney Woods class

Gravesite of Dr. and Mrs. Laurence Jones

The Plummer rock garden

Fall at Piney Woods Country Life School
Roland Freeman photos

Grace was an educated woman of modern outlook who participated in educational, philanthropic, and welfare reform activities through various organizations. To Piney Woods she brought spirit and a special concern for the advancement of her race. Her northern attitudes and experiences made her a "colored Yankee" in the eyes of the community and permittd her to bring inspiration to women and men who were still trapped by the vestiges of slavery. Her arrival coincided with the fourth successive season of crop failures due to the boll weevil and heavy rain, and Mrs. Jones saw the community first in its greatest distress.

Grace's pioneering energies focused particularly on the concerns of women. Her work, and that of others, brought the National Club Women's movement to Piney Woods. Supporters of the movement and their goals have been vividly described as

> thousands of self-sacrificing young women teaching and preaching in lonely southern backwoods for the noble army of mothers who have given birth to these girls, mothers whose intelligence is only limited by their opportunity to get at books, for the sake of the fine cultured women who have carried off the honors in school here and often abroad, for the sake of our own dignity, the dignity of our race, and the future good name of our children, it is 'mete, right and our bounden duty' to stand forth and declare ourselves and principles, to teach an ignorant and suspicious world that our aims and interests are identical with those of all good aspiring women.[37]

Mrs. Jones organized the Mothers' Club and helped local women "not only in the ways of the club, but in personal ways. They looked upon her as being some superior being because of the interest and help that she gave [them]. . . . There was most certainly a need to become involved with the women of the state who are in the rural districts . . . at the bottom of things, [without] . . . opportunities of education, travel, and libraries."[38]

Mrs. Jones's concern and compassion are fondly remembered by Leola Hughes. She recalled that under Mrs. Jones's guidance members of the Mothers' Club learned skills that would improve the home and would help their children. She met with members

Mrs. Jones organized the Piney Woods Mothers' Club through which local black women learned modern health and housekeeping practices. After her death, her ideals were carried on by the community mothers, pictured here in 1934.

for quilting parties in different homes in the county.[39] Once or twice a month, the Mother's Club met in Mrs. Jones's own home. Members came from miles around, some often walking six miles with their young children to attend meetings throughout the year, even in hot, cold, and wet weather. Pageants and demonstrations showed the women the correct way to dress a child and to make garments that the children often modeled. Mothers also learned to prepare balanced meals, including

Mrs. Jones supervised young women in basketweaving.

proper school lunches, and to weave rugs and baskets from straw.

Through the Mothers' Club Mrs. Jones organized a branch of the American Red Cross for the colored people of Rankin County that reported to the white Red Cross branch of Brandon. Though the Piney Woods branch had few members and lacked funds, its workers were fired with the inspiration and determination of their leader. During World War I they demonstrated their patriotism by contributing fifty dollars and many pairs of knitted socks and sweaters to the armed forces.

Mrs. Jones would go out of her way to help people.[40] The folks of the countryside were willing to accept Mrs. Jones's knowledge—and they shared theirs with her. For example, they offered home remedies for sciatica, of which Mrs. Jones had several attacks. Country women who came to visit suggested that Dr. Jones get "a hoodoo doctor who lived back in the woods, some thirty miles," and proposed medications that included:

Horsefly tea
Mullin and dog fennel
Mullin, mustard, and turpentine
Wear a ring of horseshoe nails
Carry an irish potato in her pocket
Three quarts of fine whiskey . . . mixed with potash and iodine
Carry a buckeye in her pocket.[41]

The Joneses listened politely to such suggestions.

Mrs. Jones's efforts in the community extended her husband's work. Her club leadership ultimately had an impact throughout the state, and the values and concerns of Piney Woods School spread far and wide.

The Piney Woods Mothers' Club was affiliated with the Mississippi State Federation of Colored Women's Clubs, which had been organized on a national level in 1895 and in Mississippi in 1903. The Mississippi federation progressed until World War I, when it experienced a decline. In 1920, however, when Mrs. Jones was elected president, delegates from twenty-one clubs were present, and at the 1923 annual meeting, held at Piney Woods, seventy-three clubs were represented.

As a part of Mrs. Jones's work reorganizing the federation, she visited thirty-six communities, working to revive old clubs and organizing many new ones. Within the federation she established the following departments: juvenile; friendship clubs of girls; education; health; music; social service; household economics; arts and crafts; reciprocity; civics; forestry; publicity; legislative; and executive board. These departments made presentations at booths during the annual meetings and distributed literature to the women. During Mrs. Jones's presidency, the home economics department presented a pageant on the proper dress for various occasions. At another time, club women in this department prepared a display of useful and attractive articles made from things generally discarded.[42]

Through the reorganized departments certain reform measures were promoted. Mrs. Melerson Guy Dunham recalled that the club petitioned the state legislature for an industrial school or home for delinquent colored girls and boys:

> It was during her [Mrs. Jones's] presidency that we started the project that ended in the training school down at Oakley.... She thought that the women should be doing something. Our motto is "Lifting As We Climb." She thought that that was one of the things that Negro women could well do, because at that time it was unheard of that you would have an institution for delinquent black boys and girls. Mrs. Bertha LeBranch Johnson, wife of the founder of Prentiss Institute, said that there was nothing on the books to prevent sending a black child to the white institution. But you couldn't find a judge in the state of Mississippi that would commit him there. So one was established for us in 1940 under Governor Paul B. Johnson, Sr. But Mrs. Jones planted the seed; Mrs. Bertha LeBranch Johnson carried it forward.[43]

Other projects undertaken during Mrs. Jones's presidency included the sale of Christmas seals to fund a colored department in the state tubercular sanitorium;[44] the obtaining of authorization from the State Department of Education to place Negro history in the curriculum of public grammar schools; the securing of permission to establish a public library for colored people in a room (or part of a room) in a public school; the initiation of a study of race relations by the white Federation of Women's Clubs; inauguration of efforts to find all blind colored children in Mississippi who might benefit from placement in an institution; and similar efforts to locate crippled black children and to submit to the state recommendations relative to their rehabilitation and education.[45]

Mrs. Jones did not depend totally upon her resources or those of Piney Woods to inspire Mississippi women. She brought before them speakers who included Robert R. Moton, president of Tuskegee Institute, and John L. Webb, grand custodian of the "Woodman" of Union Insurance Company of Hot Springs, Arkansas.[46]

The relationship of Piney Woods with the Federated Colored Women's Clubs was characterized by mutual benefit and advancement in the early days of the school's history. Piney Woods fostered many of the federation's ideas and aims, and beneficiaries of the clubs' programs—notably the colored blind, crippled, and deformed children—often joined Piney Woods's student body.

In 1913, one year after she had arrived in Piney Woods to share with her husband the living quarters in the former slave cabin, Grace Jones bore her first son, Turner. Laurence Clifton, Jr., followed, but despite the growth of her family, Mrs. Jones continued her efforts in the local, state, and national community, working in harmony with her husband.

The Jones family home, built in 1922, further extended the community spirit of Piney Woods. Community House, as it became known, served as a center for meetings of teachers, classes, and the Mothers' Club as well as for a wide range of other activities.[47] A former student at Piney Woods, Debra Gray Polk, was one of many individuals who fondly recalled Mrs. Jones's creative ways of broadening and deepening the school's relationship with the surrounding community. "I worked up in her office sometimes, though I was assigned to work in the sewing room and Art Department. She would have so much work she would get groups of girls to come and fold papers, address letters and make gifts such as hats and bags."[48]

Lennie Feazell Ross recalled how Mrs. Jones inspired her. Mrs. Jones had been the guest speaker at the New Hope County School's field day when Mrs. Ross won first prize for a shirt that she had made. After the awards had been presented, Mrs. Jones sent for her and asked her to come to Piney Woods. Mrs. Ross felt that her chance had come. She filled out the application and was accepted at Piney Woods in the fall of 1923.

Mrs. Jones also inspired groups of students in settings on the campus, outside the office and classroom. Mrs. Polk recalled Jones's work with the boys and his wife's work with the girls in Sunday school, Christian Endeavor, prayer meetings, and the YWCA.[49] In the meantime, of course, Mrs. Jones continued to travel, representing the school.[50]

After one especially long tour of eighteen months in 1927

Education for the Folks 63

Members of the Mississippi Federation of Colored Women's Clubs shown at the grave of Mrs. Laurence Jones, who had been instrumental in organizing in the group's activities.

This log cabin was built in 1939 in memory of Mrs. Laurence Jones. It served for many years as a club house for a Piney Woods faculty women's organization. (Photo courtesy of Roland Freeman)

Mrs. Jones contracted pneumonia. For a short while she was able to sit at her desk at home. Then, one day while a friend was visiting, Mrs. Jones decided to go to her office to find a pattern. Her husband found her in the cold office and rushed her, protesting, to her room. That night she went into a coma and never regained consciousness.

Mrs. Jones's passing was mourned by her family, students, and community folk, particularly the women of the state, for whom she had been a guiding light. Many people attended her funeral. They eulogized her: "Not to the dead but to the living Mrs. Jones will always belong. Here in Piney Woods the work she began will go on and on, always being a benefit to colored boys and girls."[51] She was buried under the cedar tree that had sheltered the fledgling school.

After Mrs. Jones's death in 1928, Mrs. Dunham recalled, women like "Mrs. Albert and Mrs. Bertha Dishman . . . saw to it that the club moved on at Piney Woods." During Mrs. Jones's life the Federated Colored Women's Clubs had met several times at Piney Woods, and Mr. Jones continued support of the federation until his own death.[52]

In the absence of Mrs. Jones's leadership, the spirit of the Mothers' Club seems to have declined. The Grace Memorial Club, made up of Piney Woods faculty and staff, maintained affiliation with the Federated Colored Women's Clubs, however. Local club projects included the presentation on March 8, 1938, of a play entitled *His Women Folks*.[53] Another project was the building of a log cabin in Mrs. Jones's honor. Work on this clubhouse was apparently completed in 1939, for the *Pinonian*, a student publication, reported: "'Let the women do it'—and they will show you how. This summer a commodious log house has been built down by the lake. This pretty structure will serve the dual purpose of clubhouse of the Grace Memorial Club and other school gatherings, and housing of the school's many guests when the community house rooms overflow, as they often do."[54]

3

The Students of Piney Woods

By 1919 Piney Woods School had 300 students, buildings of cement and stone, eighteen staff workers, forty head of cattle, and 1,500 acres of land.[1] The school had graduated its first class in 1918 and had become known for the opportunity that it provided to boys and girls who had no money or financial backing but were willing to work for an education.[2] At the beginning of the fifth year Jones had said: "You have come to work, to wash and iron, and sew and mend, and make brooms, and care for the mules and horses and cows and sheep, to plow and hoe and fill the barn with corn and hay and the school's commissary with meal and molasses, and to study your books and the Bible. . . . From this little country life school we expect to send out boys and girls who will be of some service in the world."[3]

The early Piney Woods students seem to have believed that formal education was the key to happy and successful living, something that their parents in most cases had not had the opportunity to secure.

Mrs. Katie Catherine Love Donnell (1906–) from Fannin, in Rankin County, Mississippi, was representative of the early students. She entered the seventh grade at Piney Woods School in 1929 at age twenty-one and left in 1937, having completed high school and enough junior college to receive a teaching training

Throughout Jones's administration students marched in groups to assemblies and to meals.

certificate. She had first learned of Piney Woods from hearing Jones speak. To earn money for uniforms and recreational fees she spent a summer working in a cousin's restaurant in Jackson. She was paid $1.50 per week, minus room and board for washing dishes and preparing food. She went to Piney Woods the following fall, paid the fees from her summer savings, and had $0.15 left for spending change.[4]

Katie Donnell had the basic qualifications for entry into Piney Woods, the desire for education and a willingness to work for it. Though students who did not have the entry fee were usually not turned away, the 1918 catalog said: "All students should come prepared to pay an entrance fee of $2.50. Every boy must bring a pair of overalls. All must bring two quilts, two pair pillow cases, two napkins, two night dresses, toothbrush, two towels, hair brush and comb. If you are coming for an education it will not be necessary to bring silk stockings and fine shoes."[5]

The wearing of uniforms at Piney Woods made it impossible to distinguish between the poor and the financially more able students. In the 1930s the girls' everyday uniform consisted of a gray dress with pleats on each side in front, beginning at the hip. The hem came three inches below the knee, and the dress had a round blue collar and black cuffs. A plain white uniform of the same pattern with a black patent leather belt and black shoes served for dress. Boys wore overalls for work and dress suits on other occasions.

In the early days some students worked all day and went to night school. By the 1940s all students worked a half day, went to school a half day, and studied at night. The academic program initially involved teaching students in largely ungraded and unstructured classes, but the school later instituted formal classes at the various grade levels. The program which had evolved at Piney Woods by 1918 grouped grade levels according to a six-three-three plan like that used in many public schools.

With the passage of time and the growth of the boarding department for high school students, the community school became almost a separate entity on the campus. The Rosenwald and Slater funds in 1923 financed construction of a new green building that became known as the Rosenwald School and housed the first six grades. It included a room for industrial training as well as one for the school lunch program, and it was used for many community functions. Some students commuted to the Rosenwald School from the local community, and (unlike the boarding school) it received whatever funds were available from the county, including teachers' salaries. It used state textbooks, for which students in about 1918 paid rental fees ranging from $3.00 to $5.00. During the Depression, book fees amounted to between $2.50 and $6.60. All students benefited from the supplementary hot lunch program, but students above the eighth grade had to purchase their books.

The Rosenwald School participated in the annual field day program toward the end of spring. It was coordinated by a county committee and in 1938 included contests of skill and exhibits of maps, drawings, business letters, and test papers. There were basketball tournaments and other athletic events.

The Rosenwald Community School was built in 1923 to house the first six grades at Piney Woods. The Rosenwald building still stands, although it is not used for classes.

Night programs were often followed by socials for the students and banquets for the teachers.

The seventh, eighth, and ninth grades formed the junior high school. The tenth, eleventh, and twelfth grades formed the nucleus of the boarding department and work program. The high school curriculum earned Piney Woods a reputation for high academic standards, although the school was not yet accredited. (At the time there were no accrediting agencies for many black schools, and often these schools did not adhere to standard academic procedures.)

In those days, Claude Phifer recalled, "many of our early teachers were not even high school graduates. . . . They went to summer school. We use to have in the various counties what they called 'Normal,' a summer school for teachers. They would go to these summer schools every year and get credits. That's the way many of them got out of high school and even college. . . ." For some, "by the time they got their B.S. degree it was time to retire."[6]

In 1917, W. F. Bond, state superintendent of education,

selected Jones to manage the state normal for colored teachers, which was held in Jackson during July.[7] The need to prepare black teachers to work in rural schools was great in the early years of Piney Woods, and Jones therefore advertised that many of his students who had finished junior high school could teach.

By 1918 Jones had invited the teachers of county schools to enter Piney Woods for normal schooling during the summer. "We are glad to give them special courses in literary or industrial work. It is a good opportunity to become efficient in the new studies required and in all kinds of industrial work."[8] In 1925 the first normal school graduates received certificates.

The two-year junior college normal training program was not established until 1931 and graduated its first class two years later. This teacher training program was run in cooperation with the Mississippi State Department of Education. Negro teachers who enrolled could concentrate on business, music, industrial arts, farming, landscape architecture, and stone sculpture.[9]

One of the two best-known programs was that in business skills and administration. So efficient were the graduates who went on to a junior year in a senior college that they often obtained jobs in the offices of the president and business manager. The music program was also known for its excellence. Students who trained in music had the opportunity to join traveling groups that included the Cotton Blossom Singers, International Sweethearts of Rhythm Girls Band, and later the Rays of Rhythm.[10]

The established programs left room for innovation and addition. In 1933 Olga Finke of New York came to Piney Woods and set up a Montessori nursery. At one time this school accommodated between 75 and 100 preschool children from the community.[11]

Piney Woods always retained the aim of making academic learning practical and relevant to the communities from which the students came.

> Arithmetic is applied in determining the cost of making cotton as against the cost of growing corn, in estimating the value of a cow by testing the milk she gives, and in determining the relative value of

Piney Woods School 70

Students at Piney Woods helped to perform all the chores of the school's farm, including hog killing.

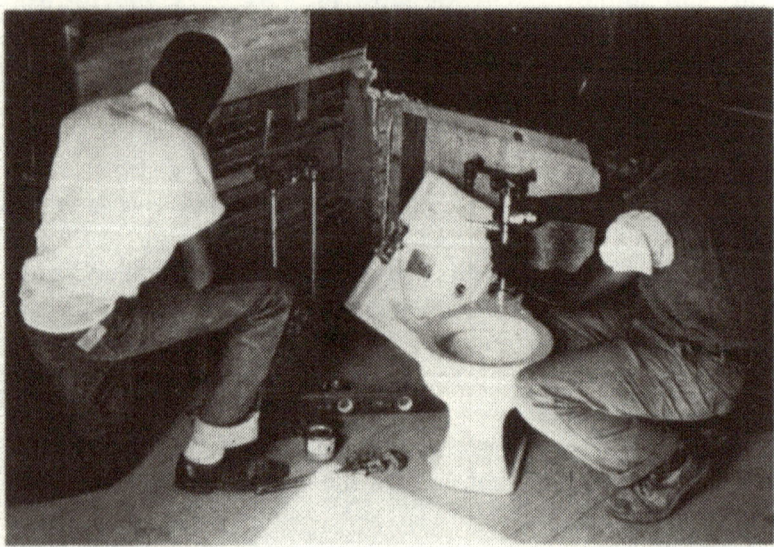

Students in the 1950s worked under a skilled plumber to learn the trade.

the Piney Woods "rooter" and a Berkshire. Chemistry is used to show that it has something to do with curing the hams of this Berkshire, with home sanitation, with the preserving of fruits and vegetables, with the making of molasses, and with the testing of seed corn. It is all a training designed to meet conditions as they are and not an effort to force upon the pupil such education as he would need were he to become President of the United States.[12]

At another time Jones wrote:

Our boys in the larger cities, and especially in the border states and the northern schools, have had the best education from their earliest years; they are the ones to become doctors and lawyers. You will make better farmers, mechanics, and other tradesmen. Do what you are best prepared to do and you will be keeping close to the ground. The girls as a rule are preparing to be teachers or to follow some trade as sewing, housekeeping, or something of the sort. In that way they are keeping close to the ground, for they are looking forward to doing that which their early training must necessarily confine them to.[13]

Lenzie Braddy's recollection of class sessions with J. D. Hardy illustrates Jones's philosophy in practice.

Every day we had to leave the auditorium and go down under the hill to the Agriculture Classroom and read *Successful Farming* and all that kind of stuff. We read a few lines and you'd see us going out across the woods spotting trees, seeing what kind of disease this tree had. Then we'd jump in his car and we'd go out to somebody's farm and look at what he had. Sometimes we would let them know that we [were] coming to see if we could help them. The next week or the same day, we'd run there and run some terraces for him to keep his land from washing off.[14]

This approach was well suited to many students' needs. Some did not continue past the eighth grade, and many came to Piney Woods at age eighteen, nineteen, and older, entering the school as third and fourth graders. Many wanted only to acquire a skill and enough academic training to find work. An advertisement in the *Piney Woods News* of 1930, 1943, and 1944 read:

Cooks and Maids With A Vision and Goal

If you do not want books or music, we have hundreds of calls from Northern and Southern wealthy families who want reliable well

A young Laurence Jones (left) led in the clearing of land to build Taylor Hall, the first building on the Piney Woods campus.

Some students learned sewing, weaving, and other forms of needle work. These activities were part of the academic program and were not considered as credit for one's work requirements.

trained help in their homes. We can train you for this kind of work. Many girls earn $50 to $75 a month clear of board and room twelve months in the year and save their money to continue their college education in large colleges, or buy a home. Write Piney Woods School, Piney Woods, Mississippi.[15]

Jones preached that the person ennobled the work and that work was never degrading. "The only disgraceful thing about toil of any kind is the half doing of it."[16] Students' lives were organized around a positive work ethic, and it was constantly reinforced during vespers or chapel service. Jones often reminded his students of what he had learned from his parents: "doing one's job was nothing more than one's daily duty to God, and beyond that lay the infinite possibilities of him who dared."[17]

This work ethic gave a certain dignity to the student's work assignments at Piney Woods, whether in the office, kitchen, field, laundry, or shop. In the early history of Piney Woods School, a "working" student had to perform "some work profitable to the school." Sewing, making baskets, brooms, needlework, and other hand-crafted objects, and agriculture were regarded as educational activities, and the time "spent [learning them] cannot be credited to working a part of the way." The educational work was reserved for the student who had $8.00 to $10.00 per month in cash to spend for tuition, board, room, laundry, electric light, and heat.

Girls performing "work profitable to the school" were assigned to the laundry room or to the domestic or business departments. The young men who were boarding students were full-work students, partial-paying students, or full-paying students and worked accordingly.

The 1918–1919 catalog explained that Booker T. Washington had made night school popular for poor boys, adding: "This school swings open its doors and says to him—'Come to Braxton, you will not have to work any harder than you have been working, we will not only give you your living and clothing for this work that you do, but will give you an education and opportunity to rise in life.'"[18]

Not all students earned their tuition at Piney Woods by working on campus. Piney Woods also permitted students to work at publicizing and raising funds for the school. Mrs. Grace Jones led the first group of traveling students in the summer of 1923. By 1926 four groups were on the road, and a group of blind singers traveled after 1932. Scheduling these groups became very complicated for the school. There were musical directors, advance agents, brochures, souvenir programs, and the problems that attend student groups traveling. The Cotton Blossom Singers were especially popular for Negro spirituals.

The International Sweethearts of Rhythm also brought the school many dollars and much publicity. This group formed in 1939 as a jazz band that played for local dances and concerts. Its members won an amateur prize on a trip to New York's World's Fair in 1940 and became full-fledged professionals in 1941. Ranging in ages from sixteen to twenty-five, the Sweethearts met a demanding schedule, usually boarding their bus immediately after evening performances, so that by morning they could have traveled several hundred miles. The girls worked hard and delighted audiences throughout the United States in large and small theaters, including the Apollo in Harlem. Other musical groups from Piney Woods that went on the road included the Rays of Rhythm and, in the late 1940s and 1950s, the Glee Club, directed by Alice Lattimore, which entertained dinner clubs, conventions, and organizations throughout the state. The musicians usually had more calls than they could accept and still continue their education.[19]

Sports were also popular at Piney Woods. Boys played soccer and football until Thanksgiving Day, afterward shifting to basketball and volleyball until February. In early spring strenuous preparation began for the season's baseball competition. Boys also played tennis and swam, and the annual community fairs included track events. Though the athletic program for the girls was less ambitious, they engaged in tennis, volleyball, basketball, and regular gymnastics.[20]

Piney Woods musical groups performed throughout the nation. Those pictured here were presenting a program in the Jackson City Auditorium in the late 1940s.

Throughout the 1920s and 1930s Piney Woods had a famous baseball team. World War II was chiefly responsible for its demise. During its heyday, however, the team played Prentiss Normal and Industrial Institute, Jackson College, Utica Institute, and even white teams such as the Piggott Merchants of Piggott, Arkansas. The Piggott *Banner* on June 2, 1933, reported: "The colored boys made a great hit here." Their pleasant dispositions, sportsmanship, and sheer ability brought them much applause. They entertained at parks and court squares accompanied by singers during their stay.[21] For many years some parts of the local, state, and national community knew of Piney Woods only through its traveling groups—the baseball team and the musicians.

In addition to the organized athletic events, Piney Woods students invented games, such as "Rap-Jacking." This was a battle game played in the evening during the summer of 1933 from 7:30 to 9:00 or until the bell rang for bedtime. Farm boys challenged campus boys, both sides dressed in three or four pairs of trousers, a sweater, and an overcoat—padding sufficient to ward off the sting of flogging with a leather belt.

With groups of men standing on each side of a dividing line, the game began. "The campus boys sought to nab a farm boy and flog him until he capitulated. Farm boys snatched campus boys trying to invade their camp and gave them such a flogging

In the early 1950s the sports program for girls included basketball.

that they would beg for mercy and retire from the field, escorted by their conquerors who would take the vanquished to the men's dormitory, where their commandant saw that they did not return." No one was generally hurt, and since the campus boys outnumbered the farm boys, they often won.[22]

By 1918 Mondays had become work days for cleaning up the campus, and Saturday, also a special day, prepared staff and students for Sunday. Nonreligious clubs met, and boys and girls found an opportunity to socialize. The bell rang at 3:30 P.M. to stop work and again at 4:00 P.M. to dismiss school. For the remainder of the day, students prepared for Sunday by cleaning uniforms, washing their hair, and polishing their shoes.

Regular Monday campus clean-up was an important facet of the students' school experience for many years.

The ringing of the bell is a long-established custom at Piney Woods, signaling wake-up time, daily activities, and bedtime. Former students heard the wake-up bell an hour earlier than the 5:00 A. M. clanging that awakens students today.

Afterward many played croquet, tennis, or baseball or read a book.

Following the Saturday evening meal there were literary, agricultural, or music club meetings and often sponsored programs for the student body. Such programs or meetings were followed by the "socials." Though socials were new to the students who came from the Piney Woods region, they resembled gatherings at many other black boarding schools of the period, particularly Utica and Prentiss institutes. Ada Adams, a student from 1922 to 1924, recalled that there was music but no dancing, not even square dancing. Of the prohibition on dancing she said, "I was one of these that had been taught many things were wrong for people to do who had accepted Christ as their personal Savior. However, as I have grown in age, I find that it is the heart that God wants and not the ways in which you do things. . . ."[23] Another student from 1929 to 1937 recalled: "They had different ones play the piano and they marched around. Then on Sunday evenings, they'd let the boys . . . write a note to whatever girl they wanted to talk to. The matron would get the note and notify the girls."[24] Reginald Hayes, a student from 1936 to 1940, remembered that

> at social times you marched with the girl instead of dancing. It was strictly a no touch deal. I mean, when I say touch, I mean catching hands and that sort of thing.
>
> Maybe it could have been a little different. I think you could have had dancing because we had the escorts. The matrons and everybody was there, so I didn't see anything wrong with them dancing together. Because we had to dance right upon a big stage in front of everyone, you know. But that didn't happen there with my dear ole friend Mother Gant. [She was a stout, jet-black head matron with a strong heavy voice, stern eyes. She limped to the right as she walked.]
>
> You just didn't be touching. You marched around, and that was about the size of it. You had your social afternoons on the campus. And oh! they had all type of people out watching to see.[25]

As in many a coeducational boarding institution, boys and girls sometimes attempted greater intimacy away from the watchful eyes of the chaperons and matrons. Hayes commented on clandestine meetings.

> I don't know about slipping off in the woods, but I know a lot of things happened. I do know there was a lot of boys that really got in the girls' dormitory. . . . I had a chance to go in but to me, I see it wasn't worth it. I know my parents would have been so disappointed in me. I was working with a guy painting. . . . We had the ladders and things right there where it wouldn't be no problem for us to go right in. But we never took the chance. . . . Not that the idea wasn't in your mind, but you just decided against it. . . . They had quite a bit, I can say, hanky-panky going. But it was nothing real bad.[26]

Nellie Bass described the accepted practice of "complimenting," whereby boys and girls exchanged notes and arranged to meet in the girls' dormitory to talk during the social hour. Occasionally they met outside, under the watchful eye of a matron.[27] This circumscribed social life was generally accepted by the early students. After all, they had come to Piney Woods by choice and primarily sought an education, which was offered to them, as we have seen, in a variety of ways.

In addition to schooling students, Piney Woods sought from the outset to encourage worship through Bible study, prayer meetings, church, Sunday school, mottos, chapel, vespers, and the group singing of Negro spirituals. Today, as in the past, the school maintains a special relationship both with the religious community of the southern Bible Belt and with groups outside its geographic area.

Although Piney Woods was always nondenominational, in the 1930s the Lutheran mission under the leadership of Rev. G. A. Schmidt sought to shape the students' religious life. Rev. Schmidt came to Piney Woods in response to a request that Dr. Jones addressed to the Lutheran Synodical Conference Missionary Board at a time when the school had no chaplain or religious instruction. At one time approximately 150 students and faculty—almost half—were members of the Lutheran mission. The Lutherans' work was greatly appreciated, but other groups were encouraged to participate in the religious life of Piney Woods.[28]

Between 1948 and 1950 or 1951 many Rankin County youth learned of Piney Woods from summer Bible camps operated by Rev. Erwin R. Weddell, a Lutheran. Students memorized Bible verses to qualify for the opportunity to spend a free week at the camp. After leaving Piney Woods, Rev. Weddell established Pioneer Bible Camp in Rankin County near Jackson and continued his program.

Other religious groups who sponsored religious instruction at Piney Woods included the Church of the Brethren, which sent volunteers to the school in the 1950s. The emissaries offered religious instruction and worked wherever they were needed in the school. For many years Piney Woods also had affiliations with the Young Men's and Young Women's Christian Associations and sent delegates to the state and national meetings. In April 1931 Piney Woods entertained the Older Boys' Conference of the YMCA, which Jones said brought together the white and colored leaders of our boys and was wonderfully helpful.[29]

In addition to serving young people of all ages who came for the day or as boarding students, Piney Woods School reached out during its history to another disadvantaged group. As president of the Mississippi Federated Colored Women's Clubs, Grace Jones had provided the initial impetus for a state school for the colored blind.[30] During 1920–1923 efforts had begun to locate all of the colored blind children of the state so that they could be placed in some institution. As a result, when a commission was established in 1928, the whereabouts of blind colored children were known. Sen. Jesse A. Adams worked untiringly on behalf of such children.[31] Thanks in large part to his efforts, the state appropriated $3,000 to start the school in 1929, and Piney Woods was chosen as a temporary site.

In addition to housing the new school, Jones was expected to find a teacher. After many inquiries he learned of Martha Morrow Foxx, a graduate of the Overbrook School for the Blind who was teaching the primary class in its summer school. Jones recommended Mrs. Foxx, and the commission readily offered her the position.[32] Mrs. Foxx had been born with impaired vision. She first attended the Raleigh School for the Blind in North Carolina and at eleven continued her education at Overbrook in Philadelphia, where her family had moved. She pursued her studies after she came to Piney Woods, developing the school and spending summers at West Virginia State College, at the University of Wisconsin, and finally at the Hampton Institute, where she received a bachelor's degree.[33]

The commission paid Mrs. Foxx the salary of fifty dollars per month, making her Piney Woods's highest paid teacher. The commission also paid Piney Woods between fourteen and twenty dollars per month as room and board for the blind children. In 1929 the school for the blind was viewed as an experiment. The first ten students were recruited throughout the state on a trial basis and ranged in age from five to twenty years old.

Mrs. Foxx arrived at Piney Woods in mid-April 1929, about three weeks before her students were expected. Recalling her first impressions, she said, "Piney Woods was really in the pioneer stage when I first went there. . . . We had outdoor toilets for the dormitories.[34] The first night, they put me in a double bed with somebody else. I never slept. I told them the next day, 'I am just not going to sleep like this. I don't want anybody to sleep with me.' This is so primitive."[35]

After the first blind students arrived, many adjustments proved necessary. Although the blind lived for a short time with the sighted students, Jones decided to provide them with a separate cottage. The first term for the blind students began in May and ended in June of the following year, when some of the children went home for vacation. A few remained at Piney Woods, where the state thought they would be better cared for.[36]

Mrs. Foxx administered not only to the children's intellectual needs but to their physical and moral needs as well.

> She washes six little boys night and morning and tucks them away in their beds. Each Saturday she gets out a big round

A school for blind students was established at Piney Woods in 1929. Blind students were able to learn practical skills for living at this school, which was the only educational institution for colored blind children in the state. Piney Woods discontinued its program when the state provided a facility in 1950.

> wash tub and gives them their weekly hot baths with the help of one or two student girls. She keeps tabs on their clothes. She instructs them in their mat-making; cane-seating; knitting, sewing and such industrial pursuits, as well as in their regular grade work. When they are sick, she anxiously watches over them just as a mother would, altho' in this she is assisted by the school nurse.[37]

One highlight of the blind students' year was a dramatic presentation, for which they learned to move on the stage like sighted persons. In 1942 a Rockefeller grant made it possible for Jones to hire Grace Halsey to assist Mrs. Foxx. That year the students staged *Androcles and The Lion*[38] for a community audience. The community folks also came to see the blind school perform a Christmas program of carols. In addition to singing, many of them played the piano well.[39]

Mrs. Foxx taught all of the blind students until they completed the eighth grade. They then entered high school with the regular students. They participated in the activities of the other students, particularly their academic subjects, and books were read aloud to them. They also continued to use the Braille method in studying arithmetic, geography, physiology, and grammar.[40]

In spite of the pioneering living conditions that she found difficult, Mrs. Foxx persevered. She taught the children social graces, including table manners, and the practical skills they needed to cope with life at Piney Woods. Jones was always supportive of her efforts, and when the state aid for the blind students' room and board was withdrawn during the Depression, he gave them the opportunity to work their way through school. At one time two quartets of blind students traveled as Cotton Blossom Singers.[41] The blind school was saved by the contributions of friends that were used as scholarships for blind students. In the spring of 1934 its first class of eighth-graders graduated.

Though the Depression curtailed funding, the commission continued to make its monthly inspection tours of the conditions for the eighteen blind students. The July 1933 inspection tour included Mrs. McBryde, Miss Mause, the homemaking teacher at the white school for the blind, one white blind student, and Senator Adams. These visitors announced that a tour conducted the following month would seek to formulate specific recommendations concerning the colored blind school that they would present to the state.

During these years of the Depression the blind students had many needs that Piney Woods could not meet without state aid. The school could not provide showers, indoor toilets, or fireproof vaults in which to store the valuable Braille library. Furthermore, in addition to the ten students that Mrs. Foxx was able to teach in 1935, there was a waiting list of more than thirty for whom facilities were totally lacking.

Not until the 1940s, when the economy began to improve, did the movement to establish a permanent school for the colored blind gather momentum. During the summer of 1940, while Mrs. Foxx was at West Virginia State, an administrator suggested that she seek help from the Public Welfare Department. She did so and was referred to Mrs. S. A. McBryde, who in turn approached Gov. Paul Johnson, Sr., who called President Roosevelt. President Roosevelt sent an official to investigate, and soon the colored blind of Piney Woods were able to sign up in Jackson to receive welfare payments. Once again the state began paying for their board and other expenses, as it had done before 1932.

The battle for legislative support was intense. National leaders in education for the blind came to help urge the Mississippi legislature to make appropriations for the school. Helen Keller spoke in the Piney Woods chapel on May 28, 1945. Her listeners included all of the colored blind then being educated in Mississippi.

> We who are blind or deaf have a peculiar problem to solve, and we know that perseverance is mightier than any other force. In all of you I sense a brave resolve to lift yourselves above harsh circumstances; and surely you will if you work long enough and persevere and believe in the abilities God has given you. It does not matter how you respond to the call to usefulness—with your brain or your hand, you will be equally happy to feel that you are part of Life's greatness.[42]

That evening, when Miss Keller spoke at the school for the white blind of Mississippi, located in Jackson since 1845, she said, "The colored are also blind, and are denied a school of their own in this state; this is still a Democracy, and the colored blind need help as much as the white."[43] She made similar statements during her tour of army and navy hospitals of the state, inspiring Mississippians to hasten completion of a public school for the blacks who were blind.

One problem was that the state legislature did not want to appropriate money for a school for the blacks without also appropriating money for a new school for blind whites. Mrs. Foxx commented:

> If they had gone on as soon as the money was appropriated, we would have had our school two or three years earlier. But they were waiting to try to find enough ground for both schools, and they had settled on building both schools on the

same campus when . . . Fielding Wright got up there and said he didn't want to have no races mixed. . . . Well, so the Building Commission got nervous, so they had to find another location instead of putting us over on Eastover [an upper-class white community of Jackson]. That's where the white school was. They wanted to put it over near Jackson College, near the College Park Auditorium.[44]

After an alternative site had been located in Jackson, the building began. The school for the white and colored blind of Mississippi was at last completed in 1950, after more than thirty years of effort. During this period Piney Woods School had provided not only the support but the determination and initiative which moved the idea forward. Furthermore it had educated the colored blind of Mississippi from 1929 to 1950 with state and private support. In its twenty-one years of existence at Piney Woods, the Colored School for the Blind represented a significant example of state and private as well as interracial cooperation in a humanitarian cause.

Helen Keller (seated, second from left) visited Piney Woods in 1945 while she was in Mississippi to promote the establishment of a state school for the colored blind. Piney Woods blind students are seated and standing around Miss Keller and other dignitaries.

As at any school, Commencement Day at Piney Woods was marked by special ceremony and significance. The large numbers of parents and white visitors who attended were always impressed with the discipline and accomplishment of the students. The poise and dignity that they showed on this occasion contrasted sharply with the singsong recitations and rude or rowdy behavior often seen on the closing day of other rural schools.

At Piney Woods, visitors on Commencement Day found a seat in the school chapel, which from the 1920s to 1973 was usually filled with guests, black and white. Graduates who had led the marching student body into the chapel reappeared, dressed to represent a skill which they would demonstrate. The May 1930 program opened with a Negro spiritual. The class motto, "We Lift as We Climb," hung at the rear of the stage, past the singers. To one side stood a piano, "next to it a table and typewriter, and so the line continues: a small press and font of type; a table of hand-woven baskets; a tiny house ready to be plastered; a gasoline-engine; then comes a brick-making machine, a kitchen range, cabinet, and table; a shallow box, six-feet square, green with growing vegetables. Then there is a rug-and-mat department, and many other things."[45]

After three spirituals, the singers retired. Edward Nelson Taylor read from a worn Bible and led the congregation in prayer. Each graduate then gave a short, succinct talk about the history and uses of a trade, with illustrations. After office workers, craftsmen, plasterers, and brickmakers, the visitor would

> hear a low voice say, "Whoa, Bill!" and looking around we behold a lad dressed in a blacksmith's apron and cap leading a horse down the broad aisle. He stops his charge near a farrier's box which we have not seen until this minute, and there before us he pares a foot and applies a shoe, showing with seeming ease what he has learned about blacksmithing.... A clicking of small hoofs [is heard] on the chapel floor and two enormous hogs, each weighing about five hundred pounds [appear]. They are docily following a young graduate of general agricultural operations, who halts his pets in

front of us and proceeds to give us a most enlightening lecture on the value of thoroughbred hogs.[46]

From such demonstrations visitors and students alike could see the pride in achievement and strength of character that Piney Woods brought forth in the black community, qualities that represented perhaps the school's most significant contribution to the state and the nation.

Piney Woods students marched to graduation ceremonies to the tunes of the Piney Woods band.

Laurence Jones introduces visitors at graduation exercises in the school chapel in the mid-1950s. Jones is assisted by his secretary, Carrie Stewart Crofton.

Students marched into Chandler Auditorium for assembly programs under the direction of Piney Woods Vice-President Singleton Bender (1909–1970).

The Students of Piney Woods 89

Student demonstrations of the practical skills learned at Piney Woods were a part of commencement programs from the late 1960s to 1974.

Jones (second from right) presents diplomas to graduating seniors in the 1960s, assisted by Singleton Bender (background, far right).

4

Support for Growth and Expansion

Although Laurence Jones founded the school at Piney Woods, its actual construction and growth, as I have shown, resulted from community effort more than from the labors of any one individual. Lumber, geese, and a piano were some of the largest gifts that the school received in its early days and helped Piney Woods to remain debt free during its first year of operation. Expansion and development plainly required funds, however, and for these Jones had to look north.

Jones eventually cultivated his connections in Iowa, but that state produced only two encouraging responses to his letters of solicitation during the school's first two years: those of Emily Howland and Asa Turner.[1] Like leaders of many other private institutions, Jones traveled north to plead his cause. Perhaps on the recommendation of his first benefactor, Edward Nelson Taylor, he soon went to Keokuk, Iowa. There he visited Lee Hammill, who remembered Taylor from the days when he was a barber there. Jones next visited schoolmates in Des Moines.[2] These contacts formed a base of support for money, materials, and teachers.

A. A. Zimmerman, a lawyer who had entered the University of Iowa the year Jones graduated, recalled, "At the first Univer-

Dressed in work clothes, Jones welcomes one of his former teachers, Iowa educator C. C. Carsten, to Piney Woods.

sity convocation in 1909–1910 school year—at the beginning of his Junior year—President George E. McLean of the University announced the founding of Piney Woods School by Mr. Jones."[3] Such public announcements planted seeds for a growing Piney Woods constituency. Superintendent Palmer of Marshalltown public schools, (including the high school that Jones had attended), led his students in collecting sixteen dollars to send to Piney Woods.[4] Student-sponsored fund-raising events such as the Elizabethtown College community chest drive also contributed funds. The first bequest was made by the Rev. Jessie Cole, chaplain of Iowa State Soldiers Home, who left his entire library to Piney Woods in 1913.[5]

Many black Iowans also contributed. The API Club, a black women's organization in Sioux City, in 1914 sent a valuable box of clothing in an effort to provide practical application to the club's motto, "Lifting As We Climb."[6] Another black, Selby Johnson from Keokuk, Iowa, gave $100.[7] Also in 1914, a woman whose mother had been a slave donated property to Piney Woods and joined Mrs. Jones's mother in coming to live at the school.[8]

Iowans black and white began moving to the school in order to give of themselves as best they could. This was the beginning of "Little Iowa" at Piney Woods. Nellie F. Brooks in the winter of 1917 became the first of many white women who came to offer their services. Other Iowans who came south included Z. E. Chandler, an academic administrator and fund raiser for Piney Woods, and Sue Riley Wolfer, one of Jones's former teachers, who joined Piney Woods in the fall of 1939.[9]

The Iowans contributed to Piney Woods in many ways. J. D. Edmundson, first suggested publication of "Our Helpers' Column" in the *Pine Torch*, which initially listed four pledges of ten dollars each from the University of Iowa and five pledges from Iowa State University. A special Iowa edition of the *Pine Torch* in November 1938 announced the planned erection of an Iowa State Memorial Building at Piney Woods. J. H. Huxford of Des Moines served as chairman of the committee appointed to raise $20,000 from 20,000 Iowans.[10]

Nellie F. Brooks (right), the first white teacher at Piney Woods, came from Iowa in 1916 to help Dr. Jones. She spent the following two winters there and traveled with the first group of Cotton Blossom singers in the summer of 1920.

Some Iowans in those early days contributed large amounts; one was Abraham Slimmer, who gave $2,000. The W. O. and E. C. Finkbines, owners of the Green Bay Lumber Company in Des Moines, Iowa, made generous gifts to Piney Woods that included 800 acres of land near the school from which the timber had been cut. The Finkbines had been fraternity fellows whom Jones had known when he waited on tables as a student at the University of Iowa.[11]

Another large contributor to Piney Woods before 1917 was George W. Dulany, who intended his gift as a memorial.

> In 1850 a Negro girl was sold in Missouri as a slave. She became the nurse for two generations of our family. We all called her "Aunt Lunky." She lived to be 86 years old. She willed her accumulated estate—about $9,000.00—to my son. I knew Laurence for about 10 years and knew that he needed a girls' dormitory. I took the Aunt Lunky bequest with additional funds from our family and asked Laurence to build the dormitory and dedicate it to our beloved "Aunt Lunky."[12]

The basement of Dulany Hall was used as a kitchen and dining room during the 1930s and 1940s. Dulany Hall, the first brick building at Piney Woods, was a gift of George Dulany.

Jones and the students and faculty of Piney Woods greet two important financial backers, A. A. Hyde (center) and his son, George Hyde, officers of the Mentholatum Company.

The Dulany family became lifelong contributors to Piney Woods. George Dulany continued to contribute funds in large amounts until the dorm was completed. Though the students at Piney Woods had begun work on this first permanent structure before World War I, it was not dedicated until 1921.[13]

Funding support for Piney Woods soon came from beyond Iowa. Outstanding contributors elsewhere in the nation included A. A. Hyde, a discoverer and manufacturer of pharmaceuticals; C. L. Dayton, who gave fruit and pecan trees; and Henry C. Muskhoff, who laid out plans for the school's grounds and long-term expansion. Other contributions came from Mrs. William H. Morris of Valdosta, Georgia, and from Jeannette James Hobby; these women gave to Piney Woods the proceeds from the sale of books they published.[14] Some donors contributed tuition funds for individual students. Estella Parish of Churubusco, Indiana, a graduate of Manchester Church of the Brethren College and the mother of seven children, adopted through correspondence and assisted three women students at Piney Woods. Her letters to the students often included three or four dollars for spending money, and she also sent needed items of clothing. In at least one instance she continued her aid during the student's college years.[15]

After the Civil War and during most of the Jim Crow era large private foundations made funds available to black southern private educational institutions. The Jeanes Fund provided the first such support for the Piney Woods program.[16] For the construction of the one-story Rosenwald School, Piney Woods received $1,000 from the Rosenwald Fund and $500 from the John F. Slater Fund. G. S. Dickerman, former administrator of the Slater Fund of New Haven, Connecticut, promoted Piney Woods while serving as general field agent for the Southern Education Board Conference for Education in the South. As a part of this effort he published "From Iowa to Mississippi," which appeared in a 1913 issue of *Crisis Magazine* and in the *Half Century Magazine* for August 1915.[17]

George Foster Peabody (1867–1915) was a charter member of

the General Education Board, serving as its treasurer in the 1920s, and was a trustee of Hampton Institute. Peabody and Jones formed a lasting personal friendship, and in later years Jones wrote to him, "You are the first and only one to become interested in Piney Woods of that great group of Eastern philanthropists who have done so much for my people."[18] The *Pine Torch* of November 1927 showed Peabody's home in the background of a photograph of Dr. and Mrs. Jones, Jones's sons, and the Cotton Blossom Singers.[19]

Peabody was convinced that vocational education was the key to the educational needs of southern blacks. In the introduction to Jones's book, *The Spirit of Piney Woods*, Peabody compared Jones with Booker T. Washington. He was impressed with Jones's sacrifice of personal opportunities and willingness to struggle with the "definite limitations and hindrances in Mississippi," where the physical, mental, and moral devastation of the Civil War was still evident.[20]

Though records of large cash donations to Piney Woods School by Peabody have not been found, it seems likely that if the Peabody Fund had not been liquidated in 1914 by a gift of $350,000 to the Slater board, Piney Woods would in time have become a large recipient of its funds. Peabody evidently suffered severe losses during the Great Depression, and his only recorded gifts to Piney Woods were two checks in the amount of $100 received in 1934.[21]

Ella Jane Carter, a Piney Woods graduate of 1918, knew Peabody in another connection. As she later recalled: "George Foster Peabody was down in this area and came to visit Piney Woods School when I was teaching here. I had charge of the academic department, so he talked with me, and visited classes. He asked me how much I really knew about southern schools."[22]

Piney Woods had sent Miss Carter to the University of Northern Iowa in Cedar Falls, Iowa, where she had received a B.A. in public school music education. When she joined the staff at Piney Woods, she knew little of southern black colleges such as Hampton, Howard, the Atlanta University system, and Talladega. After Peabody had visited he sent James Hardy Dillard, director of the Julius Rosenwald Foundation, to speak with Miss Carter. Dillard was impressed with Miss Carter's work.[23] Peabody wrote to Jones: "I am glad to have from Dr. Dillard the special suggestion respecting the advantage Miss Carter might derive from three months spent at Spelman or Hampton or some one of our schools of long experience and many friends. I hope that you will second Dr. Dillard's suggestion that we try and arrange for such an opportunity for her."[24] Jones granted Miss Carter leave for the tour, and Dillard and Peabody made up the itinerary and arranged for Miss Carter to spend about a week at each of the black institutions. She also visited Warm Springs and Columbia, Georgia, the town where Peabody had been born. According to Miss Carter, "During the Civil War when [Peabody] was a boy, a Negro man sheltered him, his mother, and the rest of the family in caves. He never forgot it."[25] Shortly after her tour Miss Carter received a master's degree from Columbia University Teachers College. She returned to Piney Woods and served as director of the academic program and teacher of music until 1941, when she went to Rust College.

The August 1938 *Pine Torch* quoted Jones as saying of Peabody: "[He] knew that right would triumph, that he rightly placed implicit faith in us, urging our advancement along trade, education and commercial lines. A philanthropist himself, his funds followed his heart, so generous checks came from him. But, best of all, was his belief in us."[26] The Jeanes Fund, the Rosenwald Fund, the Slater Fund, and George Foster Peabody were perhaps Piney Woods's only early sources of philanthropic support. It was not among the schools founded by Tuskegee graduates (such as Utica Institute) that Booker T. Washington recommended for funding. Perhaps, as Frederick D. Patterson, former president of Tuskegee, suggested, the Hampton-Tuskegee group of financiers did not feel that Jones needed their help. He retained his Iowa connections, and his school seemed to be succeeding without major foundation support.[27]

Simpson County was the first government source of funds

for Piney Woods, initially providing fifteen to eighteen dollars per month in salaries, as noted earlier.[28] The other local, state, and federal sources of support, also mentioned elsewhere in this book, may be summarized briefly for the reader's convenience. By 1923 Rankin County had begun to pay the salaries of teachers who taught at the Rosenwald School on the Piney Woods campus. This support continued until the early 1950s, when the Rosenwald School closed with the advance of the consolidation movement.[29]

The state of Mississippi paid the salary of the first teacher hired for the blind students who attended Piney Woods School from 1929 through 1950. The state also paid for the room and board of these students from 1929 to 1932. Other state payments defrayed expenses connected with the summer normal school from 1917 until sometime in the 1920s.[30] Then, too, for some years Piney Woods, like most black schools in the state, received used textbooks at little or no cost, and the National School Lunch Act provided Mississippi funds to pay for the noon meal at Piney Woods.[31]

The largest amount of federal aid to Piney Woods came when the U.S. Department of Agriculture under the Smith-Hughes Act paid the salary of J. D. Hardy in the 1920s and 1930s. In the late 1930s Piney Woods also received a contract from the Neighborhood Youth Administration to hold the vocational training camp for young women.

Although government and foundation support of Piney Woods school was meager, it helped the school in its struggle to meet the needs of the black community it served. To elicit and encourage the support of individuals far and wide on whom Piney Woods School chiefly depended for funds, however, Jones prepared an extensive publicity campaign. It stressed the school's humanitarian purpose and described the students' struggle in terms that appealed to people of even very modest means. Contributions as small as twenty-five cents were gratefully received and were added to the earnings of the traveling baseball team, bands, and singing groups. Equally important to the

Dr. Z. E. E. Chandler came to Piney Woods to teach English in 1943. She led the campaign to raise funds for the building of the library and a classroom building with an auditorium that is named for her.

school were the gifts of individuals who labored at Piney Woods receiving little or no financial compensation for their services.

Zilpha Ellen Chandler came to Piney Woods after hearing the Cotton Blossom Singers at Upper Iowa University. Although she held a Ph.D. degree in English, she accepted a reduced salary of forty dollars per month and undertook to build and house the school's first library.

In 1943 there was no library in Rankin County or in the two adjoining counties of Simpson and Smith for 8,326 black children of school age. Furthermore, there was no first-class public library in the entire state that Mississippi blacks—51 percent of the total population—could use. The only libraries to which blacks had access were those on the campuses of Jackson, Tougaloo, and Alcorn colleges.[32]

Mrs. Eley of the Mississippi Library Commission and Mrs. F. O. Alexander of the Jackson College Library described the situation at Piney Woods.

> There is no place for a library and at present the books are kept in a small, dark corner off the auditorium. The book collection consists mostly of donated books which, as you may imagine, is a sad looking lot of material better suited for scrap paper. . . . The plan for the library is that it is to serve the community as well as the school. Since such a little has been done in our state for the Negro libraries I should like to see this develop as a demonstration of the type of library service that we want for the Negroes.
>
> Dr. Chandler is devoting her life and talents to the school and the fact that she has raised $18,000 for the library in about thirteen months indicates her courage and ability.
>
> It is the policy of the Library Commission to give service to Negroes, but our appropriations have been too small to give more than advisory service. If we get the increased appropriations requested at the next session of the State Legislature, we will be able to help to some extent with books. . . .[33]

Zilpha Chandler's appeals for funds were often touching and always straightforward. One of the fund-raising circulars read: "Most of our students have never been inside a library. Imagine how they long for the privilege to enter one." An eleven-year-old girl at the school often "imagined herself going up white steps to the children's room"—but she had never seen a library.³⁴ Another circular read: "Books catalogued! A reading room! Classrooms for the blind! . . . 'Our boys will make the brick and do most of the carpentry work.'"³⁵ As the English teacher, Zilpha Chandler asked her students, including those who were blind, to write letters in their own words asking people to give donations. Jones, too, wrote letters in support of the project. "The largest sum, $8,000, was given by Mrs. Dickman, formerly treasurer at Upper Iowa University, and her brother, Milo Maltbie of New York City. Ten thousand dollars were given by a foundation of which President Jessup (SUI) was then the manager. This money was the original stock for the library."³⁶

Responses by both Northerners and Southerners to the appeals made it possible to lay the cornerstone in 1946 and to complete the library in 1948. When it was finished and stocked, $50,000 remained in the building fund and was used for the trilevel academic building that today contains Chandler Auditorium, with its balcony and stage large enough for a basketball court. After an additional six years of labor and solicitations, the academic building was completed in 1954 at a total cost of $200,000. Zilpha Chandler remained at Piney Woods until a few months before her death in 1975.³⁷

Piney Woods communicated with donors not only through fund-raising groups and letters of solicitations but through its quarterly, the *Pine Torch*, which began after Emily Howland, one of the first individuals to send the school money, suggested in 1909 or 1910 that Jones purchase a printing press and publish a newsletter.³⁸ The publication's name referred to the long walks rural blacks made

> to the church at night, through the deep piney woods, by the light of a pine torch—the one in front holding it high above his head and the rest of us trooping along behind.
>
> Pine torch is made up of slivers of fat pine—that is, pine that still has rosin and turpentine in it. Some called it lightered—I guess a contraction for light wood—not in weight

but the possibility of making a light. I discovered that two slivers would not burn but created a coating of carbon. But three or more pieces would make a torch—for the air circulating between the slivers would mean no carbon. So I got to thinking that I and my faculty could not do anything by ourselves to create light in these piney woods. However, with the help of the northern and southern friends I could make, we could together create a light—throw the torch to others. With that in mind I thought it a good idea . . . to call our school paper "The Pine Torch."[39]

Beginning in May 23, 1911, the *Pine Torch* made appeals and shared information about the school's philosophy, activities, programs, students, and progress. Between 1911 and 1920 it reprinted articles on the status of the recently freed former slaves. An article on lynchings in 1916 compared Georgia (twenty-nine lynchings during the year) with Mississippi (eleven lynchings). Other articles discussed public issues of concern to Negroes generally.[40] Readers outside Mississippi and the South learned of the impact that their contributions could make on Piney Woods.

The *Pine Torch* also printed articles about school needs. In response to one such piece, Robert J. Smart sent twenty-five dollars to provide a student with an industrial scholarhip, saying that he had not realized how much such a small sum could buy. Another article read: "Every Monday, the girls scrape the bottom of the spring trying to get enough water to wash with. Water to drink must then be carried a half mile and we have no fire protection at all, we have but little when the spring is full. Here is an opportunity for some kind friends to say as one other once said: I feel grateful to anybody who will take of my spare money and use it to such a good purpose."[41]

An early *Pine Torch* reported that the school wanted to take over a plantation which had been "worked by slaves whose remuneration was the right to live. Their children and grandchildren are now happy to work it for an education. . . . Have you ever thought that you would like to help these ex-slaves who have been free, just fifty years? These people who were once owned and traded and sold like cattle by a race with 200 years of

Piney Woods School 104

Ralph Edwards (left), host of the "This is Your Life" television program that featured Jones, visited Jones at Piney Woods.

history back of them?"⁴² An acre of land at the time cost $10.00, and the school needed $6,000 to buy 600 acres. The *Pine Torch* provided the school's most effective means of reaching the larger community. Other published efforts by Jones to publicize the school included four books between 1910 and 1935 and numerous articles. Two later books also publicized work under way at Piney Woods: Beth Day's *The Little Professor of Piney Woods* (1955) and Leslie Harper Purcell's *Miracle in Mississippi* (1956). In addition, television and radio proved useful. For many years the Piney Woods Singers were aired early on Saturday mornings by WJDX/radio. Jones's appearances on radio and television shows such as "We the People" and the "Don McNeill Breakfast Show" in 1953 drew further public attention to the school. Probably most important, however, was Ralph Edwards's program "This Is Your Life."

Jones's efforts to establish an endowment for Piney Woods dated to 1918 and launching of the Slimmer Endowment Foundation. The subsequent Piney Woods Endowment of 1929 succeeded in amassing $24,000. Both funds were depleted by the Depression, however, and by 1954 little money remained. Ralph Edwards's broadcast coverage of Laurence Jones and Piney Woods in that year gave the school the publicity it so desperately needed. During the program Edwards asked each viewer to send Jones one dollar. "The money arrived in huge mail sacks. Four days after the television program 60 sacks of money had been received. Special arrangements had to be made by the Piney Woods Post Office" and the Deposit Guaranty Bank at Jackson "to take care of the avalanche of contributions."⁴³ The money was invested in the name of the Piney Woods Foundation, which by 1957 had assets exceeding a million dollars in value and has subsequently grown with repeat showings of the program, fresh contributions and bequests, and returns on investments. The success of the "This Is Your Life" appeal was indeed a dream come true.

Piney Woods's donors have not penalized the school for its successful publicity. Contributions have swelled. Increasingly

An efficient staff helped Jones keep track of funds donated to Piney Woods. They included (LR) Eula Kelly Moman, Clarence E. Dishman, and Doris Grisham.

since 1950 individuals have given stocks and bonds; Max Fleischmann donated Standard Brands securities in large number, and a check for $50,000 was received from his estate. Madeline Kirkland of Howard University provided $15,000 for a domestic science cottage in 1958. Blanche Dulany Leuthold gave money for the Hospitality House, which provides quarters for guests. A Dallas businessman contributed money so that boys could learn upholstering, watch repairing, and radio and television repairing as well as tailoring. R. W. Millsaps of Jackson persuaded a relative, Frances Butterfield, to send the school $13,000 in 1962. Virginia Kay of Los Angeles, the editor of a column in the Pasadena *Independent*, continued to sponsor invitational events to raise money for the school.⁴⁴

Some people gave to Piney Woods because Jones's work resembled that of Booker T. Washington. It was generally believed that Jones "brought thrift and purpose into a hidden corner of the black belt, to have set Negroes raising their own corn and raising their own figs, putting their children to learning

Helping Jones to keep up with private correspondence was his personal secretary, Mrs. Carrie Stewart Crofton.

books, farming and trades.[45] Thus in the 1930s, 1940s, and 1950s Jones's name was frequently mentioned in connection with those of Washington and R. R. Moton. These educators had brought 10,000 American Negroes into step with the rest of the population.

As important as the way Piney Woods School solicited funds was its method of thanking people for their contributions. Piney Woods followed a philosophy similar to that of Estella Parish, who said: "I do not consider my contributions of any great importance to anyone but me. I firmly believe that to receive you must be willing to give, and my returns have been great."[46] So Piney Woods for years sent friends at Christmas pine and holly wreaths, sacks of pecans, and other items made by the students. The school also sent thank-you notes and receipts imprinted with the words "Investment in Humanity." Copy on the back often explained how to give bequests and educational annuities as well as survivors' bank deposits and endowment funds.

The Piney Woods spirit was not only outward but inward.

The school opened its doors offering southern hospitality to all visitors. Guests enjoyed a hot meal, often accompanied by Negro spirituals sung by students; a clean, pine-scented room to sleep in; and a leisurely, guided walking or riding tour of the campus.

5

The School in
a Changing Society

The school at Piney Woods espoused racial harmony based on Christian principles. Achievement of this goal has been a monument to the friendship possible between races when people are dedicated to the advancement of humanity without bitterness and hatred.[1] Jones used a simple prescription for humanitarian values in his relations with the local, state, and national community.

The region in which the school was located, as noted earlier, was strictly white man's country. During Piney Woods School's embryonic years there was a decline in public support for black education, lynchings increased, and Jim Crow laws and terrorist groups proliferated. In the face of these adverse forces, Jones developed a special relationship with many local whites, such as John R. Webster. As Webster later acknowledged, Jones was careful to heed the will of his white friends, seeking their advice and sanction frequently and staying away from politics.[2]

In incorporating the first board of trustees for school, Jones included two local blacks, two northern whites, and three southern whites. By serving on the board whites could constructively help blacks develop their talents and abilities. Such positive efforts to establish rapport with the white community were 99 percent successful. On several occasions, however, Jones's life seemed in jeopardy.

Webster reported that in about 1912, after Jones had brought Capt. and Mrs. Asa Turner to spend the night at his home, the local whites decided to teach him a lesson. There was talk of raising a crowd, of publicly whipping Jones, and of ordering him to return to the North. Webster wrote:

> I called in Uncle Fleet and Mr. Bill Phelps, who had known me long before I wore my first pants buttoned up in front, and who had good jobs at the mills and both of them had three sons, each employed at the mill. These two gentlemen usually had access to all the grapevine gossip round about. So I said . . . "if anything is done to Jones or that school, I will shut this mill down until every guilty party has been arrested or made to leave the country. You know what happened to that bunch that thought they would set up a whiskey business here; don't you? And you may say to those fellows that I know who they are; and I know how to reach the federal authorities".[3]

On another occasion the president of Piney Woods School found himself with a noose around his neck. Jones had gone to speak at a revival meeting about the United States's entry into World War I. Hearing phrases like "Life is a battle ground" and "We must stay on the firing line and wage constant battle against ignorance, against superstition, against poverty," two white boys who were passing by concluded that Jones was urging the church to support the Germans. The boys returned to their homes, saying, "'Speaker up 't church is urging all the niggers to rise up and fight white people.'" The next day a mob took Jones to a clearing, placed a noose around his neck, and tossed him on a brush pyre. After firing their guns in the air and otherwise trying to intimidate Jones, they permitted him to speak. By his words he succeeded in changing the crowd's mood, and at last an old man lifted the noose from Jones's neck, saying, "'Come on down, boy, we jes' made a slight mistake.'" The potential lynchers then passed the hat and collected more than fifty dollars for Jones and his school.[4] Another time "a white farmer came to a Piney Woods concert and stationed himself in the door with a shotgun. He'd heard some young white boys aimed to break up the gathering and he aimed to stop them."[5]

Though Jones escaped serious physical harm in these incidents, racism posed a blatant and ever-present threat for Jones and his students. George Hall, a student at Piney Woods in the 1920s, said:

> Race relations were very poor when Dr. Jones came. I remember passing a little town they called Bell Pine that was our little station down there where we would get off the train. We were frightened to go by or near any place where whites were playing or where they were working because they usually had a very hostile attitude towards us. I remember passing one day going down to Bell Pine where some little kids were playing. They were making mud pies, and this little white boy picked up a whole pail of water and threw it at me. Of course I felt like slapping him down, but I didn't do it because it would have meant that I probably would have been lynched or beaten half to death if I had responded in an unkind way toward this kid. That was the way it was when Dr. Jones came here.[6]

The school spent some time trying to convert the white people in the neighborhood. Hall said that in addition to Christmas caroling, students and staff would go out and sing for whites during the Easter services. "Most of the time we were singing in black churches. Eventually when the white people saw what we were doing and . . . [that we were serious,] they would invite us in their churches."[7]

In spite of the color line and Jim Crow practices in Mississippi, white groups of men and women began to want to learn more about blacks through Piney Woods. Jones and singing groups were often asked to come to white meetings, for example. They did so while carefully observing the rules of segregation and separation. Black groups entered through the back door, and if they were served, they sat not with the whites but in the kitchen or in a separate room prepared for them. At the appropriate time, the speaker and the musical group were brought into the club meeting. This was the case on one occasion when Jones was invited to speak before the white and female Mendenhall

Study Club. After club members had opened their meeting and had taken care of their business, the Glee Club sang. Jones was then introduced as one of the Negroes of the South who had greatly helped his race. When he spoke, Jones enumerated ways in which the people of Piney Woods School sought to create goodwill among the white people.[8] He noted that Piney Woods sent singers to white colleges and accepted speaking engagements to civic clubs. Further, the school used local white and black labor, bought local produce in large quantities, and tried in many other ways to create an atmosphere that fostered racial harmony.

Recognition of Jones's ability to engender goodwill found expression in 1929 when he risked personal injury in a car accident rather than hurt white women and children who had already had a car accident just minutes before. The *Brandon News* commented: "His has been a life always taking the ditch in order to do larger good in life. All of the white people of Mississippi who really know Jones are proud of him and his growing Piney Woods School and they are glad to call him friend and citizen of the South. . . . The *Brandon News*, is glad to count him among the black men of Dixie who have white souls."[9]

Piney Woods made neighborly overtures, and over the years whites of the community gave generously of their services, risking the hostility of other members of their race. In about 1933 Jones recalled "the former teacher at Braxton, who after he had gone over his mail route, came to Piney Woods each day to teach classes; [and] . . . the carpenter in the neighboring small town who, during all the years the school has stood, has come and worked when we needed him."[10] There developed a true spirit of neighborliness. One reminder of this spirit may be found in the February 1930 issue of the *Pine Torch*. A picture shows Mrs. Homer Barwick and Mrs. Will McKay of Braxton, members of the white community who rushed to help Piney Woods after a fire on January 10 which destroyed the girls' dormitory.[11] In those early days, Jones said, the Southern people of influence who aided him included members of the state Board of Education. They brought "visitors down to see our institution; they gave the benefit of their advice in matters that touched their work" and they worked for Piney Woods in all possible ways.[12]

Excerpts from the *Pine Torch* illustrate how Piney Woods spread goodwill beyond Mississippi. W. D. Baldwin of Oregon wrote on November 17, 1970:

> The Cotton Blossom Singers who came to the Methodist Church to sing and explain the program of Piney Woods were my first introduction to the Negro Race, and I have always been grateful for having had this opportunity especially now when a few of your race have not been on the positive side and seem to make the news headlines. Several of the Negro students in my class whom I taught in an elementary school in Portland were not the best either, and it would have been real easy to feel "Down with the whole Negro Race," but that first impression of those wholesome energetic students made the difference.
>
> It is my hope that there will always be a Piney Woods School helping the Blacks and Whites to better understand each other.[13]

Another letter described a different but equally important experience. After a last-minute performance by the Cotton Blossom Singers at the Mountain Grove Church of the Brethren in Missouri, D. Eugene and Eloise Lichty commented:

> The real contribution of this delegation came after their singing. Following the benediction they mingled freely with the congregation. Children were shaking the hands of their colored brethren for the first time, but with the enthusiasm of old friends. Babies found themselves in the arms of southern hospitality while mothers looked on in surprise because the babies seemed so colorblind! In a few minutes these fine Christian girls and their sponsor had done more to remove the color lines than the minister could have accomplished in many sermons.
>
> The next question arose, where will they eat dinner? None of our folks had ever entertained a Negro at the dinner table. Would we have to send them to a cafe? Would any restaurant in a town, which prides itself on having no resident Negroes, serve them? (This was before we discovered their own cooking facilities in the van.) Could the minister and his wife feed them all? We were determined to do so, if necessary. But, our worries were useless because our people came across as they usually do. Three families

invited them into their homes. Not only were they guests of the family tables, but the hostess also took the girls for rides to see the Ozark countryside. Truly it was an experience in interracial fellowship.[14]

The Lichtys related the story to an editor of the *Gospel Messager* from gratitude to Jones for his work, also hoping that their statement would help them and their church in overcoming prejudice. In like manner all groups of students—singers, bands, athletic clubs, and others—promoted the Piney Woods spirit of harmony and peace between the races.

The semiprofessional baseball team also carried the spirit of racial harmony. There were occasions when white baseball teams of neighboring towns came to Piney Woods and played with the Piney Woods team. At other times some of these white teams came just to use the Piney Woods field because its baseball diamond was the best in that section of Rankin County.

Throughout the 1950s and in the 1960s Piney Woods continued to promote racial harmony, providing an alternative to violent forces for integration and Black Power in the spirit it had shown since its founding. Still, Piney Woods could not exist in the midst of the Mississippi community without reflecting to some extent the color line and Jim Crow system prevalent in that society. The school observed all of the traditional southern customs. In the early days, for example, Jones seldom ate at the same table with southern white friends unless they insisted that he do so.[15]

Such customs drew protests from Helen Keller during her visit to Piney Woods. Though she was well received and enjoyed her stay, she wrote after her visit:

> God's presence smiled upon me in all of you. Then a shadow dimmed the light. Our faith, as you know, is nourished "by believing speech with the like-minded." So I think you will understand when I say I was grieved because you did not sit with Miss Thompson and me in the home where we had accepted your hospitality. Had I known that would happen, I would have refused to break bread and drink refreshment without you. Nothing shuts me out

from the joy of communion like the wicked, bat-eyed prejudice that breeds racial discrimination and inequality. Ever since I realized that such cruelty exists in people who are emotionally deaf and blind, I have revolted against ideas and systems that deny colored folk—or any other group or race—their rights as human beings in birth, education and equal citizenship.[16]

Regardless of any personal opinions he may have had in the matter, however, Jones knew the importance of heeding the political realities of his setting. Though both whites and blacks often attended the farmers' conferences, the commencement ceremonies, and the community fairs, a special section and separate tables were always reserved for whites, and they were always served first.

Although students at Piney Woods were usually very courteous and respectful to whites, complaints were heard on a few occasions. T. K. Webb of Florence, Mississippi, wrote the school about a student's lack of respect in addressing white people. Jones hastened to assure him that the student was penitent and that the incident would not be repeated. "I am sure she will never be that careless again as to say or do anything that even looks like she is being disrespectful."[17]

In the meantime, of course, white professors lived and taught at Piney Woods. The students seemed unaware of any impropriety and were appreciative of the instructors, whether black or white. Still, a section of the dining hall and even special tables were reserved for the white teachers, and as more white teachers came, their food was also often prepared differently and was served by the best waitresses. White staff members were chauffeured to town and were always shown the courtesies customary in the South. Although the school continued its policy of deference to the white community for years, Jones gradually began to acknowledge publicly that the times were changing.

> ... colored people [have come] to realize that they had a part to accomplish before the terrible gulf was bridged, but the white people have seen this in a clearer light. When white workers from the North first began to come to Piney Woods, we considered it

dangerous for our neighbors to learn that they were to be here permanently. Now nothing is thought of it. People who considered them members of a queer species, and certainly not fit to be associated with, now show themselves friendly and allow any differences of opinion to be passed over unmentioned.[18]

White teachers had been ordered away from other Negro schools or had been required to live off campus, Jones noted, but such was not the case at Piney Woods. A white member of the staff recalled that students and teachers worked together at Piney Woods with no thought of the color problem. She said, "We are far too busy to be concerned about who is who."[19]

Though Jones's relationship with the white community was responsible for much of his success, he was not always understood by his black contemporaries. The late B. Baldwin Dansby, former president of Jackson State University, charged Jones with playing up to the white man. When Jones came to Jackson dressed in overalls, unshaven, and with long wavy hair that fell to his shoulders, Dansby accused him of dressing in a manner that whites would find more acceptable. Jones's obvious effort to please white people caused many of his black contemporaries to look upon him with suspicion, although—as Dansby was careful to indicate—Jones was widely respected for the work he was doing at his school, and Dansby and other eminent blacks went to Piney Woods on several occasions to participate in various programs as an expression of support for Jones.[20]

In pursuing Jones's vision of racial harmony, the school reflected not only the practices of the surrounding white community but some of its beliefs as well. Like the larger society of which it formed a part, Piney Woods favored students of near-white complexion, for example. Before the mid-1950s and 1960s, generally only very light girls with long curly hair worked in the school offices, learned typing, became members of the rhythm band, or otherwise held positions of prominence as students. The darker students usually worked in the laundry or kitchen and cleaned homes.[21]

Many students showed similarly discriminatory attitudes in

A typical group of student office workers in the 1940s and 1950s.

relating to each other. Jones threatened to send away anyone who used the terms "Old Yellow Thing" or "Black and Nappy Headed." He said: "The real attributes that are worthwhile in a human being such as ability to study, ability to think, ability to translate one's thoughts into action, honesty, trustworthiness, dependability, progressiveness, ability to save, to get ahead in life, are found in black, brown, yellow or lily-white people of our race regardless of what kind of hair they have."[22]

Mary Parker Watkins, a former student, recalled some dissension between the half-white mulattoes and blacks. "They put a preference over the mulatto children . . . [A] little hatred went around within me all the while I was there . . . [because of this]. I was expecting the northern whites to make the difference. They didn't. . . . I just couldn't understand why they would make a racial thing out of us young people there and go all the way to Mexico to get them some real white Mexicans to bring there to make little objects of beauty out of them."[23]

Jones told students, however, that in spite of the "color line" they could succeed in life if they prepared themselves well. He often reminded them: "So you and I started out in life at a discount because of our color. . . . Nevertheless, I want you always to remember this: that although your color is a handicap in an external way and may hinder you in reaching the heights, there are within you possibilities that can make the favored man ahead of you know that you are in the race."[24]

Although Jones largely succeeded in keeping interracial tensions in check, some discriminatory practices persisted at the school until after the Black Power movement of the late 1960s. This last phase of the civil rights movement demanded equal opportunities for the black American, whether he or she had African Negroid features or European Caucasian features. The concept of Black Power, with its slogan "I am black and I am proud," represented the conscious, public acceptance by black Americans of their black African heritage and characteristics.

At Piney Woods there were no known marches of protest, demonstrations, or rallies. The institution was, after all, a grade school and high school located in the woods twenty-three miles away from the nearest urban center, and the absence of formal protest was probably due as much to the school's remoteness as to the discipline and hard work required by its educational program. After the mid-1950s Piney Woods ceased to grant whites special seating or other privileges not offered to blacks, and this change may be viewed as simply another step forward in the institution's continuous effort to promote respect and cooperation between the races.

When Piney Woods and Jones were both young, his concern for the surrounding local community was well known. Though Jones never lost his interest in and affection for the local people, the programs that Piney Woods School offered them gradually ceased, with the counties assuming a more direct responsibility for farm life and education. Piney Woods's most aggressive programs of direct community assistance preceded and overlapped with the first work done by black home demonstration and farm agents in Rankin and Simpson counties in the 1920s. These agents became less dependent upon Piney Woods for community contacts, relying by the 1950s more on the resources of their county offices.

Social changes occurred in the lives of Piney Woods residents as the government extended more services to them. The first such services formed part of the New Deal programs of the Roosevelt administration. Although Jones seldom mentioned changes in the local community in his speeches and writings, he occasionally acknowledged that society was different in the 1950s. He said in a May 26, 1952, commencement address at Alcorn College:

> When one gets out of work, we give him unemployment compensation—taking away the necessity for him to save and prepare for his own well being. It takes away the necessity for the jobless to develop their own traits of resourcefulness, thus making the individual weaker. . . . The welfare system led people to think that they can get the things they want without working for them . . . , which is causing more and more of our people to become human parasites. . . . Freedom isn't free. It has to be worked for and earned by individuals. . . . A free man works. A slave is worked.[25]

The forces of social change eventually relieved Piney Woods of responsibility for the education of community children. The community elementary school grades 1 through 8 were phased out about 1951 during the consolidation movement, terminating the aid that Piney Woods had received from Rankin County for community children who attended the Rosenwald School. Each county now had to educate its own students. Those in Simpson County traveled to the county school by bus, which was in most cases more convenient than walking to Piney Woods daily.[26]

The loyalties, time, and energies of members of the community began to be diverted from Piney Woods to the public schools, to which most now sent their children. However, some Piney Woods graduates, like Lenzie Braddy and Milton Weathersby, responded to pride and family tradition and continued to send their children to Piney Woods laboratory school. The laboratory school had its origin during the 1930s, when it provided an opportunity both to junior college teachers and to educate the children of Piney Woods employees and young elementary children who were always in the boarding department.

Although the consolidation movement reduced the number of its students, Piney Woods managed to survive. The summer school program was one of the few available in Rankin County or in the whole state for Negroes until the 1970s. Many students who went to the county schools during the year could study mathematics and English every summer at Piney Woods. Other subjects, such as chemistry and social studies, were offered during alternate summers, and there were always opportunities for sports, recreation, and work. In the 1960s the junior college was phased out because the demand for trained Negro teachers was being met by the state-supported junior and senior colleges. Also, it was decided that Piney Woods should concentrate on improving the quality of its elementary and high school curricula.

In the mid 1930s and early 1940s Piney Woods broadened its contacts with the community beyond as foreign students and visitors came to the campus. Throughout the period 1940–1974 Mexican and African students added an international flavor to the school's programs. The Mexicans often presented chapel talks on Mexican history and culture that were enhanced by colorful Mexican dances. Many of the international visitors were sent by the American Council on Education in Washington, D.C. During 1956–1957 visitors came from Indonesia, Martinique, Uruguay, India, Ethiopia, Brazil, Chile, Bolivia, Lebanon, Tripoli, Japan, Italy, Germany, Ireland, and many other places. The Sunday *Clarion-Ledger* on February 9, 1958, in an article entitled "Looking for the Practical," reported: "Two official Ministers of Education and a Director of Education of Iraq arrived at Piney Woods, sent by the State Department. They were on an inspection tour to survey public kindergarten, primary and secondary schools and teacher training institutions with particular emphasis on home economics and vocational training."[27]

Surrounding Jones is a group of second generation Piney Woods students from Mexico City. The parents of these students were among the first of many Mexico City children to attend Piney Woods.

Educators from less developed countries came and observed the methods used at Piney Woods. In addition, the school's faculty and staff traveled more widely than in earlier years. Z. E. Chandler spent a year in Africa, supported by the Ford Foundation, and she helped organize the Machobane Mass Agricultural College and Cooperative Union in Leribe, Basutoland. "This is a school with a philosophy identical with that of Piney Woods," she commented. In Ethiopia, Kenya, Uganda, South Rhodesia, South Africa, and Tanzania, she visited many leaders who had previously visited Piney Woods. She was received by President Julius Nyerere and in a broadcast from Dar es Salaam spoke to all of East Africa of the need for schools that could teach the people to work, to produce, and to respect labor as the only means to national economic development.[28]

The difficult problems that confronted Piney Woods in later years were sometimes unorthodox, related to the school's considerable success. Unfavorable publicity sometimes resulted, for example, when former students used the school's name to solicit

James deJornett Plummer (1872–1958), artist and gardner who created beauty at Piney Woods through constructing the rock garden and the girls' patio. (Photo courtesy of Yvonne Torrelongue)

funds that were never delivered to Piney Woods.²⁹ Such cases were exceptional, however, and many graduates later enhanced the school's image in the eyes of the community and the nation. As in the past, too, many former students returned to work on the campus. One such individual was Eula Kelly Moman, who had come to Piney Woods from Hattiesburg when she was twelve years old. After graduating she attended a business school, eventually returning to Piney Woods to work there until after Jones's death in 1975. Devoting herself completely to the school, she served as treasurer, dean of women, and official hostess.

During these later years, too, the Piney Woods campus was enriched by the labors of several staff members who were not teachers. James deJornette Plummer (1872–1958) had studied art at the Tuskegee Institute and had worked as a portrait photographer in England and Europe. In his black tam and artist's apron he was a familiar figure at Piney Woods. He created a sculptured rock garden and a patio for use by female students. There among roses he displayed his sculpture, which combined found objects. His creations were not always popular, but they remained in place with the blessings of the school president.³⁰ Another, less controversial artist was the folk wood-carver George Berry, who lived at Piney Woods during most of the 1970s with his wife and twelve children. Some of his creations sold for between $400 and $1,000 at the craft shows of Mississippi.³¹ During the last years of Jones's administration Berry shared his skill with the students by teaching a wood-carving course.

Staff and students encountered many communities through the white and black volunteers who came to work at the school. Some represented the Lutherans and the Church of the Brethren. Brethren volunteers in the 1950s included Evelyn Barksdoll of Michigan, Edna Davis of California, and Anna Crumpacker of Illinois. Their work enhanced the school's program, and they returned home to spread their enthusiasm about their experiences at Piney Woods.

By 1940 Laurence Jones had received recognition throughout the state and the nation for his work.³² Of the honors accorded

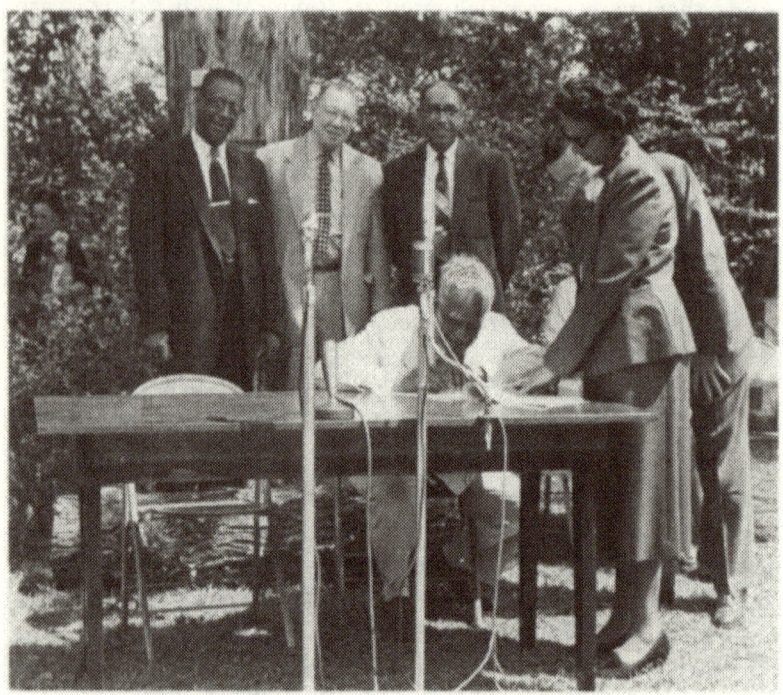

Jones, with the assistance of his sister, Nellie Bass, signs the document establishing the permanent Endowment Trust Fund, started in 1955 as a result of Jones's appearance on the "This is Your Life" television program. Standing behind Jones are (from left) Jacob Reddix, President of Jackson State College; J. R. Otis, President of Alcorn College; J. R. White, President of Mississippi Valley College.

him near the end of his life, one of the most meaningful came in 1955, when Mississippians black and white accorded him their highest praise and appreciation. At the ceremony organized by Pres. J. R. Otis of Alcorn College, white and black Mississippians sat on the same platform for the first time since Reconstruction.[33]

Jones died on July 13, 1975, and to his funeral came the community that he had so well and so faithfully served. Many of those who had first known Piney Woods as ragged orphans now returned as well-dressed citizens leading successful, professional careers. His colleagues, family, and friends laid his remains to rest on the spot where his work had begun in the Piney Woods. On November 1, 1981, six years after his death, Laurence Jones became the only black honored with a place in the Mississippi Hall of Fame.

During his last years Jones expressed great satisfaction that he had accomplished his life's ambition. He hoped that his graduates would pursue their dreams, as he had, and would eventually find peace and a sense of accomplishment. He looked to future generations to have "the proper perspective to evaluate and to reap the harvest of the potent seeds we have sown in building up Piney Woods."[34] In 1973 he expressed confidence "that the existence of Piney Woods School has caused a good change in the philosophy of the life of these people here in Piney Woods. They're more concerned that their boys and girls should have a good school and go to college, and become college graduates. They're willing to make almost any kind of a sacrifice to help in that direction."[35]

In Jones's lifetime Piney Woods opened many doors to rural blacks. Statistical analysis of eighty-five alumni questionnaires[36] indicates that early Piney Woods students had fewer opportunities available to them than today's students; whether or not the earlier group was more highly motivated, however, it certainly worked hard to succeed. As Jones noted, parents wanted a better life for their children, all of whom eventually surpassed their parents' educational accomplishments. A few biographical sketches will demonstrate how Piney Woods changed the lives of some students.

The community from which A. Brown came resembled many others in Rankin County during the 1940s and 1950s. Her family rented living space in the workers' quarters of the local sawmill. The community centers were the church and the now-defunct local Prince Hall Masonic Lodge. The greatest attraction (second only to church) was the arrival of the passenger train at Value on Sunday afternoons.

When I started school in 1944, a year before the end of World War II, I walked the six-mile round trip past the white school to and from Carter School in Brandon. In 1947 the community hired a teacher who was responsible for teaching all grades up to the fifth in the one-room local church. After a year, the attempt ended, and we went back to Carter School.

Though my father and mother had gone to Utica Institute, they never talked of sending their eleven children there. They, James Edward and Edna Mae Taylor Brown, were common laborers with an eighth-grade education. One grandparent never learned to read nor write and three of them completed the third grade. Their grandparents were slaves in Rankin and Simpson counties.

I was among the eighth graders who scored highest on the Rankin County Achievement Test that was administered by Jeanes teacher, Ernestine Pippins. For this achievement I was given a work scholarship to Piney Woods School. In the weeks following my graduation as salutatorian of my class, in 1953 my mother made the clothes that I needed to enter Piney Woods. Mrs. Pippins helped to persuade my father to pay the $25 entrance fee.

Life at Piney Woods was a refreshing change from my community and the chores of helping my mother take care of my nine younger sisters and brothers. I was assigned to work in the kitchen for a week, a day in the laundry, and then to Mrs. Carrie S. Crofton's office, where I remained and worked as a student guide and office aid, preparing the *Pine Torch* for mailing.

Though I received a B.A. from McPherson College in 1961, M.A. from Wichita State University in 1967, and a Ph.D. from the University of Kansas in 1971, my father often spoke of the importance of Piney Woods in my educational development. He said that of his eleven children, the four whom he sent to Piney Woods went on to college. He was quick to add that he was proud of all of them, but that he believed that Piney Woods was responsible for the degrees in the family.[37]

The Weathersby family in the D'Lo community of Simpson County first invited Jones to Piney Woods. Two generations of this family have attended Piney Woods, and three generations have benefited from the Tuskegee–Piney Woods tradition. The family head today is Eva Weathersby, the daughter-in-law of Forten Weathersby. She is a retired schoolteacher living on the Weathersby homestead and is active in the Jehovah's Witnesses.[38]

I heard about Piney Woods School when I was attending the city school in Jackson, Smith Robertson, living with my sister. . . . I was born in Florence, [about ten miles north of Piney Woods]. . . . Well, friends out home were telling me about trades and opportunities you could get in that respect . . . that you didn't get at the public school. . . . When you finished they'd aid you in getting a higher school.

Dr. Jones would send some of his students to the North. They'd work in some of the schools there and thereby get a higher education. Things like that interested me.

I was salutatorian of the first graduating class at Piney Woods School [1918]. . . . We didn't have a demonstration. My work was in the office with Mrs. Jones. I also taught and helped the teachers with their classes.

I haven't been too far away from [Piney Woods] since I finished. I traveled for the school soliciting funds, representing the school in Iowa and Minnesota for one year. It was quite a boost for them to have a graduate that could call upon people that had been accustomed to donating funds for the school. They could see what the school produced.

I married a man living here in D'Lo. I've lived here since finishing Piney Woods.[39]

She has taught school and later served as first assistant principal of the D'Lo School for nearly twenty years and then as an English teacher in the Mendenhall high school. After leaving Piney Woods she earned a certificate from Straight University in New Orleans, Louisiana, and completed the requirements for a degree in secondary education, majoring in English.

Her husband, S. P. Weathersby, Sr., graduated from Utica and Tuskegee institutes and had a successful practice in veterinary medicine while operating a modern farm in D'Lo for more than thirty years. At one time he owned approximately 1,000 acres of land with about 200 Hereford cattle. The Weathersbys' four children—three boys and one girl—grew up in their stucco house, which today has all the conveniences of the city home.

All four children attended Piney Woods and Tuskegee Institute. Pauline Y. Weathersby and Milton V. Weathersby graduated with honors from Piney Woods. Milton served in World War II and in the Korean War. Today he is a private practitioner of veterinary medicine specializing in large animals

Dr. Milton Weathersby, President of the National Piney Woods Alumni Association, addressed the 1978 commencement exercises.

in Simpson and Rankin counties. He is active in the Tuskegee and the Piney Woods national alumni associations and serves as a member of the board of trustees of Piney Woods School. His two children, Milton Vanzetti II and Syntyche Carola, have both attended Piney Woods School.

The other son, S. P. Weathersby, Jr., is a veterinarian with the U.S. Department of Agriculture and lives in California. On his frequent visits to D'Lo, he and the Weathersby family attend their home church, the Pine Grove Baptist Church. Jones thought highly of his abilities and considered him as a possible successor to carry on the work at Piney Woods.[40]

The Ballard family had eight children, all of whom finished high school at Piney Woods and went on to earn college degrees. Jones became a personal friend of Seth Ballard, the herb and root doctor, and encouraged him to send his children to Piney Woods. The education that they received at Piney Woods their father could not otherwise have afforded.[41]

Five of the eight children of Mr. and Mrs. Seth Ballard who attended Piney Woods.

The alumni of Piney Woods also include individuals who have achieved distinction such as Woodrow Wilson. Wilson was born on August 28, 1915, in Morton, Mississippi.⁴² He graduated in the class of 1934 from Piney Woods Junior College and was in 1966 the first black ever elected to the Nevada legislature. He was reelected for two subsequent terms, during which he sponsored the state's first fair housing bill and was a member of the Nevada Assembly education committee in 1967 and 1971.

Since 1957 Wilson has served on the Nevada State Advisory Commission on Civil Rights. As a member of the Boulder Dam Area Council for the Boy Scouts of America, he was appointed as Nevada's first black scoutmaster. He has also served as cochairman of the Institute for Black Elected Officials of the National Black Elected Officials of Washington, D.C. and on the board of advisers for the Urban Affairs Institute.

With his wife and two children he attends the Second Baptist Church of Las Vegas. He has been employed by the Nevada firm of Kerr-McGee for more than twenty-eight years. Because of his community services, he has received many honors, including the Distinguished Nevadan award from the University of Nevada in Las Vegas (1971). A Woodrow Wilson Testimonial Dinner was given for him in 1970.

Students from the earliest days of the school have remembered and appreciated the school's contribution to their lives. Some have spoken of Piney Woods in a broader context, seeing its role in increasing the opportunities available to underprivileged blacks. Claude Phifer has devoted most of his life to serving the school. After his retirement from the Piney Woods post office, he stayed on at Piney Woods as a volunteer teacher in the audiovisuals department. Though he first came to the school as an orphan, totally without family or financial resources, his service to the school has more than repaid his debt. He recalled the sequence of events that brought him to Piney Woods.

> At my home town in Yazoo City, the . . . [Federated] Colored Women's Clubs met there. Mrs. Laurence Jones was the president of the club at this time. Mrs. E. B. Miller, the wife of the late Dr. L. T. Miller, was a member of the Colored Women's Clubs and also the Dunbar Club. That's a city club there in Yazoo City. After my grandparents died, these people of Yazoo City became interested in me. They arranged with Mrs. Jones that I should become acquainted with the school.[43]

Piney Woods was a school not only for poor, orphaned, and underprivileged blacks but for the blind and the lame. One such person was a man who lacked arms. He became a teacher of economics and history. Someone else with the same handicap, Willie Weaver from Atlanta, Georgia, bought a cafe and a newspaper and magazine business. Still another, Joseph Sanders, taught in the rural schools in Mississippi. Beatrice Price was crippled by infantile paralysis; Piney Woods trained her so that she could earn a living and gave her the confidence necessary to overcome her disability. Dorothy Peacock from Charleston, Mississippi, was a midget. She entered Piney Woods in about 1952 and graduated from the junior college. Finally, Johnnie Gilmore, born in Marshalltown, Iowa, attended Piney Woods be-

Dr. Jones is pictured with the first graduating class of Piney Woods Junior College, 1933. The junior college program was discontinued in the mid-1960s.

tween 1924 and 1935. He studied music and became a drummer with the school band. As a small child he had contracted polio and had lost both legs at the age of three. He is two feet, six inches tall, his body ends five inches below his waist, and he walks on his hands. Though he is a musician, Gilmore has also become renowned for his work with handicapped and normal children.[44]

The first class to graduate from the junior college at Piney Woods demonstrated achievements comparable to those of graduates from many other institutions of higher learning. Bettye Mae Jack became the first Jeanes teacher in Scott County, Mississippi; Ishmael Jordan became a foreman in a Chicago factory; R. C. Robbins was named the principal of a school in Liberty, Mississippi; and Forest Hill achieved the rank of lieutenant in the army.[45]

Though there are glowing reports of the 1951 reunion of Piney Woods alumni, homecoming did not become an annual event until after 1974. Today, however, the school encourages former students to participate in the International Piney Woods Alumni Association. The Wade administration of Piney Woods has said that alumni help shape the school policy and make significant financial contributions. Between 20 percent and 50 percent of the school's graduates have sent their children to Piney Woods in the past twenty years.[46]

6

Past, Present, and Future

As the twentieth century gives way to the twenty-first, so do the challenges facing Piney Woods change, particularly those that relate to the survival of ethnic and racial groups in America. During his administration Laurence C. Jones led blacks through an era of racial segregation, a time during which adequate state or federal support for black education was lacking. In the last years Jones was still building relationships for Piney Woods.

John Haien, Jr., now senior vice-president for physical plant operations, came to Piney Woods in 1973 to visit his parents and later decided to stay as a volunteer for three months during the summer. At the end of that summer Jones introduced Haien to James S. Wade, the man who was to be Jones's successor.

Wade had grown up in a rural mining community in McDowell County, West Virginia, in a family with a tradition of hard work. He was the second of three children and attended the Galilee Baptist Church of Worth, West Virginia. His father, a coal miner, died when Wade was a year and a half old. One of his two stepfathers was a building contractor and at one time ran a restaurant, a barber shop, and a store. As a child, Wade said, he always tried to make his parents proud of him, "because they had always indoctrinated in us that 'we want you to grow up to be somebody.' We had a Thrift Club at school where we were encouraged to save. Each of us had banks and we would take them to the bank to open them to put money in our savings account. This encouraged us to save throughout the elementary grades. Our parents signed for us to participate. We met once a week after having saved up our pennies throughout the week. Records were kept of all deposits."[1]

Wade graduated from high school in 1936. From 1936 to 1940 he worked his way through West Virginia State College in the dining hall and office, on campus maintenance crews, and in the National Youth Administration. He said these experiences instilled in him "that if you work, know how to be punctual, how to make time, you will make it particularly with the three B's—behave, be there, and be clean. Sayings such as this by our parents and community people were pounded into us."[2]

After receiving his B.S. degree from West Virginia State College in 1940, Wade was hired in January 1941 to teach industrial arts at Champion Junior High School for blacks in Columbus. He later earned a master's degree and became principal of this school. When he accepted the presidency of Piney Woods, Wade was assistant superintendent of schools in Columbus, the highest position attained by any black in the history of the Columbus school system.

James Wade first visited Piney Woods at the invitation of Everett Reese, chairman of the school's board of trustees. Before he accepted the presidency offered him, or was introduced to the staff and students as Jones's probable successor, Wade spent a day exploring the school and speaking informally with people he met on the grounds. He accepted the position and moved to Piney Woods from Columbus, Ohio, in February 1974; John Haien, Jr., became one of his assistants.

By the time Wade assumed office, Piney Woods School had seen twenty years of profound social change, although life at the school had not suffered directly from the turmoil. The students generally remained unaware of the Black Power movement or of the emerging field of black studies. There were no programs in black history or culture like those introduced at other schools during the 1960s; Jones had said that the students' work did not leave them time to protest.[3] In its administration and operation the school remained informal, a home and a way of life for many people rather than an efficiently managed educational institution. Wade recalled that when he "first came some people at Piney Woods were concerned about whether he knew the southern mind or the southern thinking." He said that he did not see any "differences in Piney Woods and its people, and the people in Jackson" from those in Columbus, Ohio,[4] where he had worked with many Southerners who had moved north.

When Wade's administration began, the Piney Woods staff included many persons who had been there for years and were now approaching retirement age. For the first time in the school's history the board of trustees under Wade's leadership set up a retirement system with a pension for employees. The first persons to retire under this system included laborers, secretaries, and the school treasurer and dean of women, E. Moman.[5] These persons were to receive a pension as long as they lived.

Some of the retirees continued to work at Piney Woods as volunteers. Bertha Dishman offered to help with the "Lunky" on the first Saturday each month and to work one day a week as a volunteer in the office. She has also taught piano lessons, has worked in the office of the Abermarle Retirement Home, where she resides, and is presently preparing a book of photographs for the Piney Woods archives. Piney Woods sends a bus to Jackson to bring Mrs. Dishman and other volunteers to the school and to return them to their homes in the evening. Most staff members were grateful to Piney Woods for the benefits to which they were now entitled. However, many of the first to retire left reluctantly and felt some bitterness because they had been compelled to do so.

Following establishment of the benefit system, Wade set out to improve the academic program and to recruit new, trained teachers. As a result of his efforts, one year and six months later the school received Class AA accreditation, the highest recognition awarded by the Mississippi Department of Education.[6] Wade immediately proceeded to work for accreditation from the Southern Association of Colleges and Schools.

After the completion of the self-study phase in 1976, a committee for the southern region visited Piney Woods and later recommended accreditation at the annual meeting of the Southern Association of Colleges and Schools in December 1976. This certification of the educational goals, instruction, and facilities at Piney Woods meant that graduates could transfer course credits to any college in the United States.[7]

The new leadership has changed the pace of life at the school. Academic improvements have been accompanied by greater administrative efficiency. Streamlining of operating procedures has perhaps inevitably displaced the informal reliance on personal integrity, dedication, and commitment that characterized Jones's tenure.

Most volunteers hired at reduced wages have given way to professionals hired at near-competitive salaries. Mary E. G. Thomas Warren commented, "I think now the administration and faculty are able to deal with each other more on a professional basis rather than a family basis, but they are just as close-knit as ever."

By December 1978, Wade had assembled an administrative staff that he described as "one of the best I've had the opportunity to work with." This staff consisted of highly motivated professionals in various fields; two of its members held Ph.D. degrees. Wade's continuing emphasis on high professional standards has increased public confidence in the continuity and integrity of Piney Woods School.

Several members of the school's present staff have provided important links with the past. They include John Haien, Jr., who is now the senior vice-president for buildings and grounds.[8] Lucille Bender and Mr. and Mrs. Calvin Hooker have appreciated the updating of clerical operations that has resulted from the arrival of modern keypunch and data processing equipment. Mary E. G. Warren, a graduate of McPherson College who was once a member of the Cotton Blossom Singers, teaches in the elementary department and shares with the staff and student body her memories of earlier days at Piney Woods.

The mailing list of the *Pine Torch* now exceeds 3,000 names, and modern methods for timely mailing of the quarterly have been the special concern of Marvel Turner, vice-president for business affairs. A graduate of Jackson State University and a certified public accountant, Turner improved the effectiveness of Piney Woods publicity by contracting for professional lettershop (mail) services. The modern accounting department that he developed implemented an internal control system and provides the administration and supporters of Piney Woods with quarterly financial statements and budget reports prepared by computer.[9] In December 1977 the school hired its first professional fund raiser, John Bernard Jones, a graduate of Bluefield State College, who holds a Ph.D. in school administration from the University of Pittsburgh.[10]

The present vice-president of the academic department is Samuel McGee, who holds a Ph.D. in education administration from the University of Southern Mississippi. His department has worked to improve students' performance on standardized tests. Volunteer teachers have played a significant role in this effort.[11]

Today's students at Piney Woods interact with the community less than their predecessors did. The school continues to participate in the annual Mississippi fair, but students usually attend community events as spectators rather than as participants. They do participate in high school competitive sports such as basketball, however.

President Wade commented on Piney Woods's place in the changing community and suggested goals for the future.

> Many of the people in the community have passed on, and their children have moved out. I wouldn't say that the community is a dying community, because there are still many people there, but

Piney Woods School is not able to do as much as it did in yesteryear due to the fact of integration, because some people are sending their children to the regular public schools.

In the early days they were not able to go to any other school than Piney Woods after a certain grade level, but now the students are permitted to go to integrated schools. Take Mendenhall, for example. Parents have a tendency to send their children where it's most economical. It is a matter of their child walking up the street and going to school and being able to come home for lunch; they will do that rather than spend some funds to send them to Piney Woods School. So . . . now we are beefing up our programs to make Piney Woods School the kind of school that will attract students to come here and want to come and want to learn. I believe when we get to that place, we'll have what you call a school whose enrollment will show all segments of our society. We have that in our staff and we can have that in our student body. The doors are open to all students regardless to race, creed, color or sex.[12]

Though the school has no direct community program today, its relationships with local citizens are positive.

The school's financial condition is now excellent. The board of trustees has been charged with managing and investing the school's funds through institutions such as the First National and Deposit Guaranty banks. When Wade's tenure began, the investment portfolio was estimated to be worth $7 million; by 1978 the comparable figure was $12 million.[13]

In 1975 the board of trustees established the Laurence C. Jones Foundation from memorial gifts. The proceeds from this fund help replace outdated facilities as well as providing buildings to meet new needs. In March 1977 the fund had a balance of $179,000. Two modern buildings, the automotive training center and the swine barn, have been added to the campus with this money.[14]

As in the past, gifts still arrive from outside sources. Dr. and Mrs. K. R. O'Neal recently donated a registered Angus bull, affectionately known as Black Watch Alganon. Recent years have also seen corporate gifts. The Ford Motor Company gave the school a cut-away engine, and the Eli Lilly estate donated more than $3 million, part of which financed a new boys' dormitory.[15] The efforts and support of people within and beyond the school have enabled Piney Woods to expand and to improve the quality of its service to an ever-widening community.

The challenge identified by Laurence Jones when he founded Piney Woods School was the creation of an educational program suited to the needs of rural blacks in Mississippi and of the larger community to which they belonged. Jones's program succeeded in part because it did not threaten existing social and political values, and much of Jones's greatness as an educator stemmed from his profound awareness of the balance to be maintained. Despite his sense of accomplishment, however, Jones saw that more work remained to be done. "We can't stop now and say that we have reached the goal," he said. "There is still much, much to do. In fact, we have only touched the outer rim of what is needed."[16]

Jones's school during its history has seen vast changes in American society. It was founded at a time when educational opportunities for blacks were severely lacking in Mississippi, and the community provided the first resources for creating them. Today Piney Woods is less involved with the local community—but today, too, a range of educational facilities exists for black children, and many of the community needs that Piney Woods sought to meet are being addresssed through welfare programs.

It remains to consider the role that the school could and should have in the future. Development of an agricultural extension program would certainly involve staff and students once again with the lives of its rural neighbors. Still, acquisition of the necessary technological expertise and of modern farm machinery might strain the resources of Piney Woods in other areas. A more appropriate alternative might follow from reaffirmation and reapplication of the school's time-honored values. If Piney Woods is to continue to serve the constituency for which it was created, it might seek new ways of recognizing and helping the underprivileged in our society. By doing so the school could perpetuate its tradition of strengthening the "bottom rail." An important part of such a program would be continued assistance for the poor black children of Mississippi. These students need access to the school whether or not they can afford its tuition. At the same time, they—and all children—should learn to take pride in their ability to advance as a result of their own efforts, to pay their way in life.

The technological advance of an increasingly complex society does not reduce the fundamental importance of a child's sense of accomplishment in raising livestock or produce and exhibiting at a county fair. Perhaps a greater place should be made at Piney Woods not just for a 4-H Club but for other character-building organizations—the Girl and Boy Scouts of America, Y Teens, the YM and YWCAs, and Junior Achievement. Nationwide clubs can also extend to less privileged Americans many experiences that are familiar to boys and girls of greater affluence in other parts of the country. Today's youth do not necessarily have the same unfulfilled needs as their counterparts of fifty years ago. Perhaps students in the 1980s need to experience caring, affection, and strong role models as much as they need a sound academic education. In these areas Piney Woods's traditional resources and educational philosophy could serve the modern world well.

The school is also admirably equipped to stimulate pride in regional and national folk traditions. At a time when renewed interest in folklore is sweeping the country, Piney Woods could encourage knowledge and appreciation of the past in students by means of festivals and workshops in crafts and in the old-time arts of practical living. In addition, old-fashioned industry might suggest new ways of teaching basic skills and principles that are slighted by some advanced and superficial educational methods. Perhaps the best preparation for adult entry into modern society would equip each student with both practical skills in demand in the marketplace and a broad understanding of the nature of those skills and of the possibilities their mastery affords. Such an education would be strengthened by an awareness of the satisfactions to be gained from hard work. New traditions and techniques can complement the old ones. The past need not be cut off but may be built upon, so that the new and the old support each other. Some traditions may be valuable and worth retaining as they provide a sense of place—roots—and an awareness of the richness in the black heritage at Piney Woods.

Today's youth, like their predecessors, must prepare to go back to their communities, but they must also look forward to a world of vastly greater human mobility. They may be employed, for example, in a space lab or below the sea, and commuting may mean flying to Tanzania and returning to America in time for an evening activity. Piney Woods can prepare students to meet these challenges and many others as yet unknown. The idea of educational service for the underprivileged should flow as sap in the cedar tree under which Piney Woods held its first class in 1909.

If the methods of industrial education are still useful means of strengthening the bottom rails of our society, could they perhaps be productively employed in the Third World? As the Third World struggles to industrialize, it faces a growing need for a highly trained work force. The Piney Woods experience has shown that industrial education holds promise for less developed nations, and the school's doors might increasingly be opened to students from other countries. The program at Piney Woods has, after all, plainly demonstrated its practical value in preparing children for life as adults in a technological age. Then, too, if Third World youth can be led into modernity, could not the cycle of welfare dependency in America be broken by inculcating children at an early age with the traditional values of Piney Woods? By these means the pine torch might be passed from our generation to the next.

Notes

Introduction

1. Laurence C. Jones, *The Bottom Rail: Addresses and Papers* (New York: Fleming H. Revell, 1935), p. 7.
2. Booker T. Washington, et al. *The Negro Problem: A Series of Articles by Representative American Negroes of To-Day* (Miami: Mnemosyne, 1903), pp. 9–29, 33–75. Contributors included B. T. Washington, W. E. B. DuBois, Paul L. Dunbar, Charles Chestnutt, and others.
3. Thomas Jesse Jones, *Negro Education: A Study of the Private and Higher Schools for Colored People in the United States*, vol. 1 (Washington, D.C.: U.S. Government Printing Office, 1917), p. 10.
4. James D. Anderson, "Education as a Vehicle for the Manipulation of Black Workers," *Work, Technology, and Education: Dissenting Essays in the Intellectual Foundation of American Education*, ed. Walter Feinberg and Henry Rosemont, Jr. (Chicago: University of Illinois Press, 1975), pp. 38–39.
5. August Meier, *Negro Thought in America, 1880–1915*, (Ann Arbor: University of Michigan Press, 1970), pp. 85–97; *Encyclopaedia Britannica*, 1970 ed., s. v. "Pestalozzi, Johann Heinrich."
6. Meier, *Negro Thought in America*, pp. 85–97; and *Encyclopaedia Britannica*, 1970 ed., s. v. "Fellenberg, Phillip E. Von."
7. Robert Samuel Fletcher, *A History of Oberlin College* (Ohio: Oberlin College, 1943), pp. 34–35.
8. Blanche B. Coggan,, et al., *Pioneer Afro American Educator: Prior Foster, First Afro American to Found and Incorporate an Educational Institute in the Northwest Territory*, (Lansing: By the author, 1969), p. 2; Laurence C. Jones, *Piney Woods and Its Story* (New York: Fleming H. Revell, 1922), pp. 31–32; Leslie Harper Purcell, *Miracle in Mississippi: Laurence C. Jones of Piney Woods* (New York: Carlton Press, 1956), pp. 8–9. These sources conflict about Prior Foster's relationship to Jones. His sister Nellie Bass confirmed on May 28, 1982, that Prior Foster was their uncle.
9. Edith Ann Talbott, *Samuel Chapman Armstrong: A Biographical Study* (New York: Negro Universities Press, 1969), p. 155; Samuel Chapman Armstrong, *Hampton Institute's Annual Report, 1868–1878* (Hampton, Va.: Hampton Institute, 1878), p. 3.

10. Henry Allen Bullock, *A History of Negro Education in the South* (Cambridge, Mass.: Harvard University Press, 1967), pp. 5–13. James M. McPherson, "White Liberals and Black Power in Negro Education, 1865–1915," *American Historical Review* 75 (June 1970), pp. 1357–86; Meier, *Negro Thought in America*, pp. 85–97.
11. Ullin Whitney Leavell, *Philanthropy in Negro Education* (Nashville: Peabody College, 1930), pp. 156–158; Meier, *Negro Thought in America*, pp. 90, 91–92, 95–98.
12. Mildred Williams et al., *The Jeanes Story: A Chapter in the History of American Education, 1908–1968* (Atlanta: Southern Education Foundation, 1979), p. 99; Leavell pp. 149–168.
13. Claude Phifer, interview, April 23, 1973, pp. 19–20.

1. A School Comes to Piney Woods

1. Jones, "Piney Woods School," *Southern Workman*, 60 (January 31, 1931), p. 20.
2. James Loewen and Charles Sallis, eds., *Mississippi Conflict and Change* (New York: Pantheon Books, 1974), pp. 15–26; Richard Aubry McLemore, ed., *A History of Mississippi* vol. 1, (Jackson: Mississippi College and University Press of Mississippi, 1973), p. 525; Patti Carr Black, *Mississippi Piney Woods: A Photographic Study of Folk Architecture: An Exhibition at the Mississippi State Historical Museum* (Jackson: Mississippi Department of Archives and History, 1976), pp. 4–5.
3. McLemore, pp. 493, 525.
4. John R. Webster, "Memories," *Pine Torch*, February 1937, pp. 2, 4.
5. Ibid., p. 2.
6. Ibid., pp. 2, 4.
7. John R. Webster, *A Brief Historical Sketch of the Early Days of Piney Woods School* (Piney Woods: Piney Woods School, n.d.), p. 2.
8. Benjamin T. McCullough, Mayor of Braxton, interview, July 19, 1979, p. 22.
9. "Braxton," in *Hometown Mississippi*, comp. James F. Brieger (Jackson: By the author, 1980), p. 438.
10. Tommie Nathan Spencer, interview, December 29, 1978, pp. 2, 12–13.
11. Mary Jenness, "A Home-Made School in the Deep South," in *Twelve Negro Americans*, (Freeport, N.Y.: Books for Libraries Press, 1936), p. 103.

12. Leola Hughes, interview, April 26, 1973, p. 8.
13. Ibid., September 5, 1978, pp. 7–10.
14. Nellie F. Cox and Rosie Brooks, interview, September 6, 1978, pp. 20, 21.
15. Jones, *Piney Woods and Its Story*, p. 125.
16. Debra Gray Polk, interview, June 14, 1973, p. 5.
17. Hughes, interview, April 26, 1973, pp. 16–17.
18. Laurence C. Jones, interview, April 25, 1973, pp. 1–2.
19. "Took the Highroad and Found Success," in *Chautauqua: The Worth-while Kind*, Lecture Series Announcement (Independence, Iowa: Redpath-Vawter Chautauqua System, June 1918) p. 8; Beth Foagles Day, *The Little Professor of Piney Woods: The Story of Professor Laurence Jones* (New York: Julian Messner, 1955), p. 60.
20. *Mississippi Population, 1800–1970: Statistical Summary* (Jackson: Marketing and Development Department, Mississippi Power and Light, August 1970); Brookings Institution, Institute for Government Research, *Report on a Survey of the Organization and Administration of State and County Government in Mississippi* (Jackson: Research Commission of the State of Mississippi, 1932), pp. 517–18, for the general attitude on black education.
21. *Pine Torch*, February 1912, p. 4; "To Live in Hearts We Leave Behind Is Not to Die," *Pine Torch*, July 1911, p. 1.
22. Jones, *Piney Woods and Its Story*, pp. 34–35, 36–39; Jones, *The Bottom Rail*, p. 11.
23. Jones, *Piney Woods and Its Story*, pp. 15–26; Day, pp. 12–13.
24. Jones, *Piney Woods and Its Story*, pp. 24–25.
25. Day, p. 13; Jones, *Piney Woods and Its Story*, pp. 26–32; Coggan, p. 6.
26. Jones, *Piney Woods and Its Story*, p. 32.
27. Jones to Registrar of Iowa University, September 4, 1903, University of Iowa Archives.
28. Laurence C. Jones, interview, February 23, 1974, pp. 6–7.
29. Laurence C. Jones, "Piney Woods School," p. 20. Vol. 60.
30. "Jones Speaks on Tuskegee," *Iowa Citizen*, May 7, 1906.
31. Jones, *Piney Woods and Its Story*, p. 49.
32. Ibid., pp. 49–50.
33. Emily Herron (Secretary to the Principal of Hampton Institute) to Jones, May 9, 1907, Hampton Institute Archives.
34. Jones, *Piney Woods and Its Story*, pp. 48–49; Jones, "Piney Woods School," p. 20.
35. Ibid.
36. Eva Weathersby, interview, June 27, 1973, p. 5.

37. Jones, *Piney Woods and Its Story*, pp. 52–53; Booker T. Washington to Jones, *Pine Torch*, October 1913, p. 1.
38. Purcell, p. 23.
39. Hughes, interview, April 26, 1973, p. 8.
40. Jones, *Piney Woods and Its Story*, pp. 56–57.
41. Ibid., pp. 63–64; Day, p. 40.
42. Webster, *A Brief Historical Sketch*, p. 6; Day, pp. 26–27.
43. Webster, p. 6.
44. Ibid. p. 7.
45. Ibid. p. 8.
46. Ibid. p. 9.
47. Day, pp. 43–45; Jones, *Piney Woods and Its Story*, pp. 67–68.
48. Day, pp. 38–42.
49. Day, pp. 48–50; the *Rankin County Deed Index, 1886–1910*, shows ten parcels of land being deeded to E. N. Taylor, books 52, 55, 59, 67, 70, 75, 51.
50. Jones, *Piney Woods and Its Story*, pp. 69–70; Day, pp. 49–52.
51. Day, p. 54.
52. "Another Early Day Story of Piney Woods School," *Pine Torch*, December 1954, p. 4; *Pine Torch*, July–August 1955, p. 3.
53. Jones, *Piney Woods and Its Story*, pp. 71–72.
54. Purcell, p. 35.
55. Day, p. 57.
56. *Pinonian*, 1927, p. 2; Day, pp. 57–61.
57. Jones, *Piney Woods and Its Story*, p. 74.
58. Nellie Cox, interview, September 6, 1978, pp. 7–8.
59. Jones, *Piney Woods and Its Story*, p. 75.
60. Ibid., pp. 80–82.
61. *Pine Torch*, April 1912, p. 3.
62. Jones, *Piney Woods and Its Story*, p.
63. Jones, "Piney Woods School," p.

2. Education for the Folks

1. Williams, p. 97 (copy of the certificate of incorporation of Negro Rural School Fund).
2. Ibid. Booker T. Washington at Tuskegee Institute and Hollis Burke Frissel of Hampton Institute and their successors in the trust were appointed by Miss Jeanes as trustees in perpetuity of the $1,000,000 fund. Laurence C. Jones, interview, April 25, 1973, p. 13.
3. Williams, pp. 140–146.
4. Ibid. pp. 56–68.

5. *Pine Torch*, July 1911, p. 3.
6. *Pine Torch*, February 1912, p. 1.
7. Ibid.
8. *Pine Torch*, March 1912, p. 2.
9. *Pine Torch*, March 1912, p. 3.
10. "Committee of the General Education Board Conference on Negro Education," July 8–10, 1915, p. 5 (Library of Congress).
11. *Pine Torch*, February 1917, p. 3.
12. "Negro Educator Warns Race against North," *Pine Torch*, March 1917, p. 2, the [Jackson] *Clarion-Ledger*.
13. Jones, *Piney Woods and Its Story*, pp. 142–143.
14. Ibid. p. 142.
15. Purcell, p. 73. In 1917 the Piney Woods newsletter printed news of the "Dixie Farmer"; *Pine Torch*, July 1917, p. 2.
16. *Encyclopedia of American History*, 1953 ed., s.v. "Smith-Hughes Act"; Ada Carter Adams, interview, June 21, 1973, pp. 1–4.
17. Robert E. Lee, interview, June 5, 1981. "Making Good," *Pine Torch*, April 1940, p. 1.
18. Ibid.
19. "4-H Boys," *Pine Torch*, November–December 1949, p. 2.
20. "Extension Work," *Pine Torch*, March 1926 (Farm Issue Special), p. 2.
21. "Successful Year in Agriculture with Negro Project, Boys at Piney Woods School . . . Despite Conditions, 1924," *Pine Torch*, September 1925, pp. 1–2.
22. Lenzie Braddy, interview, September 5, 1978, pp. 1–8.
23. "Piney Woods Fair, Bigger and Better," *Pine Torch*, November 1933, p. 1.
24. Nelson Antrim Crawford, "The Little Professor of Piney Woods," *Rotarian*, October 1945, pp. 20–21.
25. "Mrs. Mabel Carney's Visit," *Pine Torch*, January 1933, p. 1; "A Little Journey Through Piney Woods School" (a leaflet describing Mrs. Mabel Carney's visit), n.d.
26. Leo M. Favrot, "How the Small Rural School Can More Adequately Serve Its Community," *Journal of Negro Education* 5 (1936), pp. 433–34.
27. Jones, *Piney Woods and Its Story*, pp. 124–125.
28. Ibid; Day, pp. 127, 133;
29. *Pine Torch*, June 1932, pp. 1–2; *Pine Torch*, November 1932, pp. 1, 4; February–March 1933, p. 1; October 1934, p. 1.
30. *Pine Torch*, December 1921, pp. 1–2.
31. Rosie Brooks is the third person participating in Cox, interview, September 6, 1978, pp. 29–30.

32. Polk, interview, June 14, 1973, p. 4.
33. "Christmas at Piney Woods," *Pine Torch*, November-December 1949, p. 1.
34. Jones, *Piney Woods and Its Story*, pp. 127-129.
35. Ibid, pp. 128-129.
36. "Superstitions of Southern Folk," *Pine Torch*, November 1930, p. 3.
37. Gerda Lerner, ed., *Black Women in White America: A Documentary History* (New York: Random House, 1973), p. 442. Josephine St. Pierre Ruffin, (1842-1924), delivered the address at the National Conference of Colored Women, 1895.
38. Jones, interview, April 25, 1973, pp. 14-15.
39. Hughes, interview, April 26, 1973, p. 15.
40. Melerson Guy Dunham, interview, July 3, 1974, p. 5.
41. "Remedies for Sciatica," *Pine Torch*, January 1917, p. 1.
42. Mrs. Laurence C. (Grace) Jones, *What the Mississippi Women Are Doing: State Federation of Colored Women's Clubs of Mississippi* (Braxton: Mississippi State Federation of Colored Women's Clubs n.d. [1925?]), p. 7; Purcell, pp. 66-70.
43. Dunham, interview, July 3, 1974, p. 3.
44. The sanitorium was located at Magee, Mississippi; Purcell, pp. 66-67.
45. G. Jones, *What the Mississippi Women Are Doing*, pp. 11-12.
46. Ibid. p. 6; Alferdteen Harrison, *A History of the Most Worshipful Stringer Grand Lodge* (Jackson: Stringer Grand Lodge, 1977), pp. 75-76.
47. *Fifteenth Anniversary Call for 1926* (Piney Woods: Piney Woods School, 1926), p. 8.
48. Polk, interview, June 14, 1973, pp. 3-4.
49. Ibid., p. 7.
50. Laurence C. Jones, interview, April 25, 1973, p. 14.
51. *Pine Torch*, April 1928, p. 1.
52. Dunham, interview, July 3, 1974, p. 4.
53. *The Echo, Piney Woods* March 1938 p. 3; *Pinonian*, 1939, p. 3.
54. "The Grace Memorial Club," *Pine Torch*, June 1938, p. 4.

3. The Students of Piney Woods

1. Jones, *Piney Woods and Its Story*, p. 132.
2. *Important Facts about Piney Woods* (Piney Woods: Piney Woods School, n.d. [1958?]), p. 13.
3. Jones, *Spirit of Piney Woods* (New York: Fleming H. Revell, 1931), p. 25.
4. K. C. Love Donnell, interview, October 14, 1978, pp. 2., 5-8.

5. *Piney Woods Catalog, 1918–1919*, p. 4.
6. Claude Phifer, interview, April 23, 1973, p. 20.
7. *Pine Torch*, July 1917, p. 1; Purcell, pp. 56–57.
8. *Piney Woods Catalog 1918–1919*, back page.
9. *Piney Woods School News*, vol. 3, no. 5, (1943); vol. 4, no. 1, 1944.
10. Ibid. vol. 4, no. 1, 1944.
11. "Montessori Nursery School at Piney Woods since 1933," *Pine Torch*, December 1933, p. 2.
12. C. O. Baker, *Trading Molasses for Learning* (Piney Woods: Piney Woods School, n.d.), p. 6; Jones, *Piney Woods and Its Story*, p. 137.
13. Jones, *The Spirit of Piney Woods*, p. 31.
14. Lenzie Braddy, interview, September 1978, p. 3.
15. *Piney Woods News*, vol. 3, no. 3 (1943), p. 2; vol. 2, no. 1; (1930) p. 1; vol. 3, no. 6 (1944), p. 3.
16. Jones, *Piney Woods and Its Story*, p. 139.
17. Jones, "Love of Knowledge," *Guideposts: A Practical Guide to Successful Living*, October 1960, p. 22.
18. *Piney Woods Catalog, 1818–1819*, back page.
19. Peter Suskind, "Sweethearts Band Hard Workers," *Journal and Guide*, Richmond, June 20, 1942; Lou Holloway, interview, March 15, 1979, pp. 15–16; *Piney Woods News*, 1944, p. 1.
20. *Pinonian*, 1935, p. 1.
21. Piggott (Arkansas) *Banner*, June 2, 1933.
22. Gertrude Macy, "Rap-Jacking at Piney Woods," *Pine Torch*, June 1933, p. 2.
23. Ada Adams, interview, June 21, 1973, p. 6.
24. Donnell, interview, October 14, 1978, p. 14.
25. Reginald Hayes, interview, October 14, 1978, p. 9.
26. Ibid., p. 10.
27. Nellie Bass, interview, July 5, 1979, pp. 24–25.
28. *Lutheran Mission at Piney Woods School* (n.p., n.d.).
29. Jones, *Bottom Rail*, pp. 43, 60.
30. Purcell, pp. 66–68; 119.
31. Jones, *Bottom Rail*, pp. 49, 64; Day, pp. 156–7.
32. Martha Morrow Foxx, interview, October 27, 1974, p. 6.
33. *Red and White, 1971–1972 Yearbook of the Overbrook School for the Blind*, Philadelphia: Overbrook School, 1972), pp. 28–31.
34. Foxx, interview, October 27, 1974, pp. 22–23.
35. Ibid., p. 25.
36. Ibid., p. 35.
37. "Cooperation with Government, State, and County Agencies in the Interest of Education for the Blind," *Pine Torch*, July 1933, p. 2.

Notes   149

38. Purcell, p. 122.
39. Foxx, interview, October 27, 1974, p. 19.
40. *Pine Torch*, July 1933, p. 2.
41. *Pine Torch*, July 1932, pp. 1–2; *Pine Torch*, July 1933, p. 3.
42. "Helen Keller Visits Piney Woods," *Pine Torch*, July–August 1945, p. 3.
43. "Helen Keller Pleads for New Blind School," *Clarion-Ledger*, May 29, 1945.
44. Foxx, interview, October 27, 1974, pp. 14–15.
45. Clarence Orvel Baker, *Trading Molasses for Learning* (Piney Woods: Piney Woods School, n.d.), p. 9; *Our Campus*, 1930 (unnumbered pages).
46. Baker, p. 10; *Pine Torch*, May 1921, p. 4; *Pine Torch*, June 1921, p. 1; *Pine Torch*, July 1922, p. 4; *Pine Torch*, May 1923, pp. 1–2; *Pine Torch*, May 1926, pp. 1–3; *Pine Torch*, May 1929, pp. 1, 2, 3; *Pine Torch*, May–June 1947, pp. 1, 3.

4. Support for Growth and Expansion

1. Jones, *Piney Woods and Its Story*, pp. 70, 75, 80; Day, pp. 70, 87, & 95.
2. Jones, *Piney Woods and Its Story*, p. 78. Purcell, pp. 41–42.
3. A. A. Zimmerman to the Editor, *Pine Torch*, January–March 1969, p. 1. The letter also indicated that Zimmerman entered the University of Iowa the year that Jones graduated.
4. *Pine Torch*, January 1913, p. 4.
5. "Our First Bequest," *Pine Torch*, October 1913, p. 1.
6. "The API Club Aids Piney Woods School," *Pine Torch*, May 1914, p. 1. "Lifting As We Climb" was a National motto to the National Federation of Colored Women's Clubs.
7. *Pine Torch*, December 1919, p. 2.
8. *Pine Torch*, August 1914, p. 1.
9. *Pine Torch*, December 1918, p. 1; *Pine Torch*, November–December 1939, p. 2; *Pine Torch*, May 1917, pp. 1–3.
10. *Pine Torch*, November 1938, pp. 2–4; *Pine Torch*, January 1, 1917, p. 4.
11. *Pine Torch*, January–March 1920, pp. 1, 4.
12. *Pine Torch*, October–December 1966, p. 1; *Pine Torch*, January–March 1920, pp. 1, 2.
13. *Pine Torch*, July 1916, p. 1; *Pine Torch*, March 1921, pp. 1, 3.
14. Jackson *Daily News*, August 27, 1970, Section C, and Novem-

ber 9, 1978, Section E; also Jeanette J. Hobby, *Down Memory Lane* (Dallas: Story Book Press, 1950).

15. Estella Parish to Alferdteen Harrison, January 18, 1979.

16. Jones to Dr. J. M. Dillard, July 29, 1930, General Education Board Collection, Library of Congress; Williams, p. 99.

17. G. S. Dickerman, "From Iowa to Mississippi," *Crisis* 6 (July 1913), pp. 137–40; *Pine Torch*, September 1923, p. 3, contains the May 31, 1923, financial report.

18. Jones to George Foster Peabody, October 27, 1931, Peabody Papers, Library of Congress.

19. "George Foster Peabody's Home," *Pine Torch*, November 1927, p. 1.

20. George Foster Peabody, Introduction, *The Spirit of Piney Woods*, by Laurence C. Jones, pp. 3–6.

21. Leavell, pp. 83–94; Secretary of George Foster Peabody to Jones, April 19, 1932, and March 26, 1934, Library of Congress.

22. Ella J. Carter Jackson, interview, March 2, 1974, p. 9.

23. "Dr. J. M. Dillard of Jeanes . . . Slater Fund Visits Piney Woods," *Pine Torch*, May 1934, pp. 1, 2; "George Foster Peabody Visits Piney Woods School," February 1934, *Pine Torch*, pp. 1, 2, 3;

24. G. F. Peabody to L. C. Jones, April 17, 1934, (Peabody Papers) Library of Congress.

25. Jackson, interview, March 2, 1974, pp. 1–12.

26. "A Friend to the Ages," *Pine Torch*, August 1938, p. 3.

27. Frederick D. Patterson, interview, November 28, 1978, pp. 10–12.

28. Jones, *Piney Woods and Its Story*, pp. 71–72.

29. Daniel L. Rankin, interview, July 17, 1979, pp. 5–9.

30. Jones, *Piney Woods and Its Story*, p. 124; *Pine Torch*, July 1917, p. 1; Mississippi Department of Education Superintendent W. F. Bond asked Jones to manage the state normal for colored teachers in Jackson during July and August 1917.

31. Marvel Turner, interview, December 27, 1979, pp. 23–24; *National School Lunch Program* (Washington, D.C.: U.S. Department of Agriculture, 1977).

32. Chandler's handwritten, unpublished and undated notes, in the Piney Woods Archives, gave a figure of 2,000 southern white donors.

33. Eunice Eley to American Library Association, Mississippi Library Commission: Jackson, August 18, 1945.

34. Undated circular signed by Chandler, in the Piney Woods Archives.

35. Illustrated circular soliciting funds for the library, spring and summer 1945, in the Piney Woods Archives.

36. Quoted from Chandler's notes (undated).
37. Ibid.
38. On Emily Howland, see *Piney Woods and Its Story*, pp. 75, 80; Day, pp. 70, 87, 96.
39. *Pine Torch*, April–June 1976, p. 3.
40. *Pine Torch*, May 1913, p. 3; *Pine Torch*, April 1914, pp. 1, 2; *Pine Torch*, February 1916, pp. 1, 3; *Pine Torch*, November 1916, p. 3; and *Pine Torch*, February 1917, pp. 1–2.
41. Robert J. Smart to Jones, published in *Pine Torch*, January 1916, p. 1; *Pine Torch*, January 1917, p. 3.
42. *Pine Torch*, January 1913, p. 1.
43. "TV Audience Gives $628,484 to Negro School in Mississippi," *Nation's Schools* 55 (March 1955), p. 142.
44. "What He Saw He Liked," *Pine Torch*, April–June 1966, p. 1; *Pine Torch*, October-December 1966, p. 1; "What Do Your Own People Do to Help You?" *Pine Torch*, October-December 1968, pp. 1, 3; "Professor John H. Sears," *Pine Torch*, January-March 1962, p. 1; *Pine Torch*, July-September 1962, p. 4; *Pine Torch*, October-December 1962, p. 1; Virginia Kay Rovers, Editor of a column "Just In the Family" in the Pasadena (California) *Independent*, March 17, 1968; *Pine Torch*, December 1971, pp. 3, 4.
45. *Chautauqua: The Worthwhile Kind* p. 8; "From a Southern White Lawyer," *Pine Torch*, April-June 1961, p. 3.
46. Estella Parish to Alferdteen Harrison, January 18, 1979.

5. The School in a Changing Society

1. "State Surprises African Students, Africans Visit Here," newspaper clipping, n.p., n.d. (in the Piney Woods Archives).
2. Webster, *A Brief Historical Sketch*, p. 28.
3. Ibid. p. 24.
4. Jones, *Piney Woods and Its Story*, pp. 111–113.
5. *Pine Torch*, April-June 1970 (reprinted from the *Clarion-Ledger*, October 12, 1969).
6. George Hall, interview, April 22, 1973, p. 7 Mary Thomas (Warren), interview, p. 7.
7. Ibid., p. 8.
8. "One Answer," *Pine Torch*, July-August 1954, pp. 1–2.
9. "Laurence C. Jones Averts Accident," Brandon *News*, September 26, 1929.
10. Jones, *Bottom Rail*, p. 15.
11. *Pine Torch*, February 1930, p. 1.
12. Jones, *Bottom Rail*, pp. 14–15.

13. W. D. Baldwin to Jones, *Pine Torch*, April-June 1971, p. 4.
14. Eugene Lichty and Eloise Lichty, "Experiences with Color," *Pine Torch*, November-December 1954, p. 2.
15. Zilpha E. Chandler, "Mr. Jones of the Piney Woods School: Three Boys, Coming to Him to Get Some 'Larnin,' . . .," *Iowa Alumni Review*, October 1951, p. 21.
16. Helen Keller to Jones, June 3, 1945, *Pine Torch*, July-August 1945, p. 4.
17. Jones to T. K. Webb, November 19, 1945, Piney Woods Archives.
18. Jones, *Bottom Rail*, pp. 15–17.
19. Chandler, "Mr. Jones of the Piney Woods School," p. 21.
20. Baldwin Dansby, interview, June 1973, pp. 1–4.
21. Rosie G. Bilbro and Mary Parker Watkins, interview, October 25, 1978, pp. 5–7.
22. Jones, "Color and Hair," chapel talk (Piney Woods: Piney Woods School, n.d.).
23. Bilbro and Watkins, interview, October 15, 1978, pp. 5–6.
24. Laurence C. Jones, *The Spirit of Piney Woods*, p. 65.
25. Laurence C. Jones, "Back to Lincoln," (Commencement address delivered at Alcorn College, Alcorn, Mississippi, May 26, 1952), pp. 10, 11, 15.
26. Rankin, interview, July 17, 1979, pp. 5–10.
27. "Looking for the Practical," *Clarion-Ledger*, February 9, 1958.
28. "Our Dr. Chandler on Sabbatical Leave in Africa," *Pine Torch*, January–March 1963, p. 1.
29. *Pine Torch*, July 1927, pp. 1, 3; *Pine Torch*, September 1917, p. 4.
30. Yvonne Terrelongue to A. Harrison, February 20, 1979; Lawrence A. Jones, interview, February 10, 1979.
31. George Berry, personal communication, March 1978; Dudley Marble, "Carving Is a Medicine for Piney Woods Professor," *Jackson Daily News*, June 7, 1973.
32. Laurence C. Jones, interview, April 25, 1973, pp. 12–15. In addition Jones served on the state board of the Mississippi Public Welfare Food Assistance Expanded Food Distribution Program. Also see "You Should Know Laurence C. Jones," *Sunshine Magazine*, August 1969, pp. 7A–8A; Jones became a member of the magazine's editorial board.
33. "Dr. Jones to Be Honored at State-Wide Program, January 23," *Mississippi Enterprise*, January 15, 1955.
34. Laurence C. Jones to John O. Martin, June 19, 1967; Piney Woods Archives.

35. Laurence C. Jones, interview, April 25, 1973, pp. 2–7.
36. Questionnaire prepared by A. Harrison and mailed to all Piney Woods alumni for whom addresses were available between October and November 1978. Tabulated responses are on file at the Jackson State University Archives.
37. A. Brown, interview, October 15, 1978.
38. Eva Weathersby to A. Harrison, November 1979.
39. Eva Weathersby, interview, June 27, 1973, pp. 1, 2, 3.
40. Weathersby to A. Harrison, November 1979; "The Weathersby Family," *Pine Torch*, April–June 1968, pp. 1–2; Sylvanus P. Weathersby, interview, October 14, 1978, p. 38.
41. "Ballard Family," *Pine Torch*, October–December 1967, p. 1.
42. Woodrow Wilson to A. Harrison, November 1978.
43. Phifer, interview, April 23, 1973, p. 1.
44. *Sepia*, December 1957, pp. 28–30.
45. "Reminiscing on Homecoming Day at Piney Woods," *Pine Torch*, March–April 1952, p. 2.
46. Administrative questionnaire prepared by A. Harrison, completed by Bernard Jones, Piney Woods School, May 1979.

6. Past, Present, and Future

1. James S. Wade, interview, December 28, 1978, pp. 12–17.
2. Ibid., p. 19.
3. Jim Nesbitt, "Piney Woods Pupils Too Busy for Trouble," *Press Telegram*, January 13, 1967.
4. Wade, interview, December 28, 1978, p. 23.
5. Ibid., p. 33
6. "Piney Woods School Planning for Recognition by the Southern Association of Colleges and Schools," *Pine Torch*, January–March 1976, p. 1.
7. "Piney Woods Receives Accreditation," *Pine Torch*, January–March 1977, p. 1.
8. Susan Puckett, "Piney Woods School Survives with Community Help," *Clarion-Ledger*, December 24, 1978; Wade, interview, December 28, 1978, p. 36; ibid.; John Haien, Jr., interview, December 27, 1978, pp. 12, 27–28.
9. Marvel Turner, interview, December 27, 1978, pp. 4, 8, 11–17. Turner was hired in August of 1976 and resigned in June 1982.
10. John Bernard Jones, interview, December 27, 1978, pp. 1–12, 32–38. J. B. Jones was hired in December 1977 and resigned in May 1981.

11. Samuel McGee, interview, December 29, 1978, pp. 1, 19–21. McGee resigned in May 1980; he had been hired in about August 1978.

12. Wade, interview, December 28, 1978, pp. 28–29.

13. Ibid., p. 32.

14. "New Buildings Added to Piney Woods," *Pine Torch*, January–March 1977, p. 1; "1975 at Piney Woods School: A Year of Reflections and Progress," *Pine Torch*, October–December 1975, p. 2.

15. *Pine Torch*, April–June 1976, p. 3; Wade, interview, December 28, 1978, p. 34.

16. Laurence C. Jones, interview, April 25, 1973, p. 15.

Sources

Archives

This study has relied most importantly on materials available in the Piney Woods Archives. Chief among these was the *Pine Torch*, the school's quarterly newsletter, which began publication in 1910. Its contents have varied somewhat over the years (during its first two decades it often reprinted articles of general interest to southern blacks that had appeared in other publications), but its chronicle of events at Piney Woods has retained the quality of a family newsletter. Other student publications that were particularly helpful included the *Piney Woods School News*, the *Piney Woods Post*, the *Pinonian*, and the *Piney Woods Echo*. The archives also contains a useful collection of catalogs, class books, yearbooks, president's reports, anniversary calls, correspondence, photographs, and publicity materials.

Documents pertaining to the history and growth of Rankin and Simpson counties are available at the Mississippi Department of Archives and History and at the Mississippi Research and Development Center, both in Jackson. The Mississippi Library Commission has copies of the *Eleventh Biennial Report of the Mississippi State Library Commission, 1945–1947*, and correspondence relating to efforts to fund the Piney Woods library.

The Iowa State Historical Society manuscript collection, in Iowa City, has materials relating to the founding of Piney Woods, and the University of Iowa's holdings include documents relating to Laurence Jones's career as well as an excellent collection of local Iowa newspapers. The archives at Hampton Institute, Hampton, Virginia, and at Howard University's Moorland-Spingarn Research Center, in Washington, D.C., provided sources useful in tracing the history of industrial education in America and the development of black institutions of higher learning. The Library of Congress, Manuscript Division, houses the Booker T. Washington Papers and the George Foster Peabody Papers; the former collection contains sections of correspondence relating to the activities of the General Education Board and to the administration of the Jeanes and the Rosenwald funds. The Peabody Papers shed considerable light on the funding of educational facilities for blacks in the late nineteenth and early twentieth centuries.

Oral History Sources

I made extensive use of interviews on file in the Jackson State University Library in Jackson, Mississippi. The collection includes fifty-nine oral history interviews and supplementary tapes on Piney Woods School that I recorded. A photocopied guide ("Listing of Oral History Interviews of a Black School's Community Relationships: Piney Woods") is available. The Jackson State collection also houses oral history materials of a more general nature, and their use by scholars is facilitated by a catalog and by summaries of and indexes to the transcriptions.

Writings of Laurence C. Jones

"Back to Lincoln." Commencement Address Delivered at Alcorn College, Alcorn, Mississippi, May 26, 1952.
"The Best Advice I Ever Had." *Reader's Digest* 69 (December 1956), pp. 167–8.
The Bottom Rail: Addresses and Papers on the Negro in the Lowlands of Mississippi and on Inter-Racial Relations in the South during Twenty-five Years. New York: Fleming H. Revell, 1935.
A Candle of Understanding. Piney Woods: Piney Woods School, n.d. (reprinted from an unidentified source).
"Color and Hair." Chapel talk. Piney Woods: Piney Woods School, n.d.
Commencement Address. Delivered at Lane College, Jackson, Tennessee, June 4, 1933.
(Ed.) *A Day of Good Deeds*. Litchfield, Ill.: Sunshine Press, 1939.
"Demonstrations at Piney Woods." *Nation's Schools* 23 (April 1939), p. 47.
(Ed.) *Little Journeys to Piney Woods School, Piney Woods, Mississippi*. Memphis: C.A. Davis, n.d.
"Love of Knowledge." *Guideposts: A Practical Guide to Successful Living*, October 1960, p. 22.

"Miracle of Piney Woods." *Ebony* 10 (October 1955), pp. 36–41.
Piney Woods and Its Story. New York: Fleming H. Revell, 1922.
"Piney Woods School." *Southern Workman* 60 (January 1931), pp. 20–23.
"Piney Woods School—A Way of Life." Unsigned manuscript. Piney Woods: Piney Woods School, n.d. [1960s?]. (Jones's authorship is not completely certain)
The Spirit of Piney Woods. New York: Fleming H. Revell, 1931.
Up through Difficulties. n.p., 1910.

Other Sources

Anderson, James D. "Education as a Vehicle for the Manipulation of Black Workers." In *Work, Technology and Education, Dissenting Essays In The Intellectual Foundation of American Education*, ed. Walter Feinbert and Henry Rosemont, Jr. Chicago: University of Illinois Press, 1975.
Armstrong, Samuel Chapman. *Hampton Institute's Annual Report, 1868–1878.* Hampton, Va.: Hampton Institute, 1878.
"The Audience Gives $628,484 to Negro School in Mississippi." *Nation's Schools* 55 (March 1955, p. 142.
Baker, Clarence Orvel. *Trading Molasses for Learning.* Piney Woods: Piney Woods School, n.d.
Bergmann, Leola Nelson. *The Negro in Iowa.* Studies in Iowa History. Iowa City: State Historical Society of Iowa, 1969.
"Black Man Mississippi's White People Respect." *Color*, April 1957, pp. 12–15.
Black, Patti Carr. *Mississippi Piney Woods: A Photographic Study of Folk Architecture: An Exhibition at the Mississippi State Historical Museum.* Jackson: Mississippi Department of Archives and History, 1976.
"Braxton." In *Hometown Mississippi*, ed. James F. Brieger. Jackson: By the author, 1980.
Brookings Institution, Institute for Government Research. *Report on a Survey of the Organization and Administration of State and County Government in Mississippi.* Jackson: Research Commission of the State of Mississippi, 1932.
Brown, Ruth W. "New Library at Piney Woods." *Library Journal* 77 (June 15, 1952), p. 1052.
Bullock, Henry Allen. *A History of Negro Education in the South.* Cambridge, Mass.; Harvard University Press, 1967.
Butterfield, F. W. "Nothing Traditional about Commencement at Piney Woods." *School Management* 18 (June 1949), pp. 26–27.

Carney, Mabel. "Desirable Rural Adaptations in the Education of Negroes," *Journal of Negro Education* 5 (1936), pp. 439–447.

Chandler, Zilpha Ellen. "Citizen Builder." *Pioneer* 13 (November–December 1950), pp. 3–5.

———. "Mr. Jones of the Piney Woods School: Three Boys Coming to Him To Get Some 'Larnin', Opened a Highway to Education for Their Race", . . . *Iowa Alumni Review*, October 1951, pp. 20–22.

———. "Pupils Safely Face Real Life Situations." *Safety Education* 31 (September 1951), pp. 16–17.

———. "What A Student Should Learn in School besides Books." Toronto: The School, [1950].

Coggan, Blanche B. et al. *Pioneer Afro-American Educator: Prior Foster, First Afro-American to Found and Incorporate an Educational Institution in the Northwest Territory*. Lansing: By the author, 1969.

Crawford, Nelson Antrim. "The Little Professor of Piney Woods." *Rotarian* 67 (October 1945).

Crofton, Carrie. "The Boy From Missouri." Piney Woods: Piney Woods School, n.d.

Day, Beth Foagles. *The Little Professor of Piney Woods*. New York: J. Messner, 1955.

"Der schwarze Pestalozzi von Piney Woods: Nerin E. Gun erzaehlt die Geschichte der ersten Neger-Universitat im Staat Mississippi" *Schweizer Illustrierte Zeitung*, Juni 13, 1955, pp. 10–11.

Dickerman, G. S. "From Iowa to Mississippi." *Crisis* 6 (July 1913), pp. 137–40.

Dictionary of Education: Foundations in Education. New York: McGraw-Hill, 1959.

Dubois, William E. Burghart. *Souls of Black Folk*. Greenwich: Fawcett, 1961.

Embree, Edwin R. "Education for Rural Life." *Journal of Negro Education*, 5 (1936), pp. 439–47.

Emmerich, J. O. "Under a Cedar Tree at Piney Woods." Piney Woods: Piney Woods School, n.d.

Encyclopaedia Britannica. 1970 ed. S.v. "Fellenberg, Phillip E. von."

Encyclopedia of American History. 1953 ed. S.v. "Smith-Hughes Act."

Favrot, Leo M. "How the Small Rural School Can More Adequately Serve Its Community." *Journal of Negro Education* 5 (1936), pp. 430–38.

Fletcher, Robert Samuel. *A History of Oberlin College from Its Foundation through the Civil War*. Oberlin: Oberlin College, 1943

"Golden Savings." *Deeds and Data* (Deposit Guaranty National Bank), August 1969.

Graebner, Theodore. *The Light of Faith: Stories of Men and Women Who Adorned the Christian Faith*. n.p., n.d. [1923?].
Harmon, Francis. "What a Southern White Man . . . Thinks of the Piney Woods School." Piney Woods: Piney Woods School, n.d.
Harris, Ruth M. "We Come To Git Educated." *Liberty Magazine*, 1944, n.d.
Harrison, Alferdteen. *A History of the Most Worshipful Stringer Grand Lodge: Our Heritage Is Our Challenge*. Jackson: Stringer Grand Lodge, 1977.
Hobby, Jeanette J. *Down Memory Lane*. Dallas: Story Book Press, 1950.
Holtzclaw, William H. *The Black Man's Burden*. New York: Neale Publishing, 1915.
James, Doris. *My Education at Piney Woods*. New York: Fleming Revel, 1937.
Jenness, Mary. "A Home-Made School in the Deep South." *Twelve Negro Americans*. Freeport, N.Y.: Books for Libraries Press, 1936.
Johnson, Charles S. *Statistical Atlas of Southern Counties: Listing and Analysis of Socio-Economic Indices of 1104 Southern Counties*. Chapel Hill: University of North Carolina Press, 1941.
Jones, Grace Allen. "The Desire for Freedom." *Palimpsest*, May 1927, pp. 153–63.
———. *Spirit of Aunt Lunky*. Piney Woods: Piney Woods School, n.d.
———. *What the Mississippi Women Are Doing*. State Federation of Colored Women's Clubs of Mississippi. Braxton: Mississippi State Federation of Colored Women's Clubs, n.d. [1925?].
"Jones Speaks on Tuskegee." *Iowa Citizen*, Iowa City May 7, 1906.
Jones, Thomas Jessie. *Negro Education: A Study of the Private and Higher Schools for Colored People in the United States*, 2 vols. (Washington, D.C.: U.S. Government Printing Office, 1917).
Leavell, Ullin Whitney. *Philanthropy in Negro Education*. Nashville: Peabody College, 1930.
Lerner, Gerda, ed. *Black Women in White America: A Documentary History*. New York: Random House, 1973.
"Library Service to the Colored Race." *Mississippi Library News*, September 1953, pp. 112–119.
Loewen, James W. and Sallis, Charles, eds. *Mississippi Conflict and Change*. New York: Pantheon, 1974.
Loper, Ralph E. *The Lesson from the Red Bird*. Piney Woods: Piney Woods School, n.d.
Lutheran Mission at Piney Woods School. Piney Woods: Piney Woods School, n.d.
McLemore, Richard Aubry, ed. *A History of Mississippi*. vol. 1, Jackson: Mississippi College and University Press of Mississippi, 1973.

McPherson, James M. "White Liberals and Black Power in Negro Education, 1865–1915." *American Historical Review* 75 (June 1970), pp. 1857–86.

———, et al. *Blacks in America: Bibliographical Essays*. New York: Doubleday, 1972.

Meier, August. *From Plantation to Ghetto*. New York: Hill and Wang, 1976.

———. *Negro Thought in America, 1880–1915: Radical Ideologies in the Age of Booker T. Washington*. Ann Arbor: University of Michigan Press, 1970.

Meier, August and Rudurick, Elliott. *Along The Color Line: Explorations in the Black Experience*. Chicago: University of Illinois Press, 1976.

Mississippi Population, 1800–1970: Statistical Summary. Jackson: Mississippi Power & Light Company, August 1970.

"A Monumental Life Has Left Its Mark." *Sunshine Magazine*, November 1975, p. 3A.

Morrow, Sara Sprott. "Dr. 'Piney Woods' Jones." *Message Magazine*, May 1953, pp. 13–16.

National School Lunch Program. Washington, D.C.: U.S. Department of Agriculture, 1977.

"Goal $1,000,000." *Time* Magazine, January 3, 1955, p. 53.

"Piney Woods School Adds Buildings as Telecast Brings One-Half Million Dollar Gifts." *RCA Baton: News of Significant Developments in Home Entertainment Electronics*, January–February, 1957, p. 5.

Plumb, Beatrice. "The Little Professor of Piney Woods." *Christian Herald Magazine*, 1950.

———. *Lives That Inspire*. Minneapolis: T. S. Denison 1962.

———. *Lord Breathe On Me*." Piney Woods: Piney Woods School, n.d.

A Pictorial History of the Tiger Band, under the Direction of Consuella Carter. Coahoma Junior College and Agricultural High School, n.d.

Poems and Songs about Piney Woods School Honoring Laurence C. Jones and Piney Woods School. Memphis: C. A. Davis, 1975.

Purcell, Leslie Harper. *Miracle in Mississippi: Laurence C. Jones of Piney Woods School*. New York: Coment Press, 1956.

Red and White. 1971–1972 Yearbook of the Overbrook School for the Blind. Philadelphia: Overbrook School, 1972.

Rogers, Tommy W. "The Piney Woods Country Life School: A Successful Heritage of Education of Black Children in Mississippi." *Negro History Bulletin*, vol. 39, no. 6 (September–October 1976), pp. 611–14.

———. "The Dream of Hope." *Today in the New South*, May–June 1974, pp. 12–13, 16.

Schatz, Walter, ed. *Directory of Afro-American Resources.* New York: R. R. Bowker, 1970.
"The Story of Piney Woods: It's Told Today by Our Guest, Laurence C. Jones." *A. J. Clubber* (Peoria Advertising & Selling Club), September 30, 1957, p. 1.
Talbott, Edith Ann. *Samuel Chapman Armstrong: A Biographical Study.* New York: Negro Universities Press, 1969.
"This Is a Life Applauded by $600,000." *Rotarian* 86 (March 1955), p. 29.
Thompson, Ray M. "The Tender-hearted Tornado." *Inn Dixie*, March 1960, p. 16.
"Took the Highroad and Found Success." In *Chautauqua, The Worthwhile Kind.* Lecture Series Announcement. Independence, Iowa: Redpath-Vawter Chautauqua System, June 1918.
"Unique School for Blacks Started with a Log, a Dream, a Dedicated Man." *Hattiesburg American*, April 15, 1979.
Washington, Alethea H. "The American Problem of Rural Education." *Journal of Negro Education* 5 (1936), pp. 420–29.
Washington, Booker T. et al. *The Negro Problem: A Series of Articles by Representative American Negroes of To-Day.* Miami: Mnemosyne, 1903.
Webster, John R. *A Brief Historical Sketch of the Early Days of Piney Woods Schools.* Piney Woods: Piney Woods School, n.d.
Who's Who in America. 1936–1937 ed. s.v. "Jones, Laurence C."
Williams, Mildred et al. *The Jeanes Story: A Chapter in the History of American Education, 1908–1968.* Atlanta: The Southern Education Foundation, 1979.
Wilson, Charles H. R. *Education for Negroes in Mississippi Since 1910.* Boston: Meador Publishing, 1947.
Wolfe, Karl. "Great Man—Dr. Laurence Jones." *Journal of Mississippi History*, May 1976, pp. 199–212.
"You Should Know." *Sunshine Magazine*, August 1969, pp. 7A–8A.

Index

Abolitionists, 9
Academic learning, 3, 69, 135
Accreditation of black schools, 11, 68, 136
Achievement Tests in Rankin County, 126
Adams, Ada, 78
Adams, Senator Jesse A., 80, 83
Addison, Michigan, 8
Africa, 121
Africans, 10; students, 120
African heritage, 118
African Methodists Episcopal Church, 9
African Negroid features, 118
Agricultural classroom, 71
Agricultural colleges (schools), 8, 9, 40
Agricultural extension system, 43, 46
Agricultural Department, United States, 43, 44, 46, 99, 128
Albert, Mrs. mentioned, 62
Alcorn College, 11, 40, 101, 119
Alexander, F. O., Jackson College librarian, 101
Alumni Association, International Piney Woods Club, 132
American Baptist Home Mission, 9
American Council on Education, 120
American Missionary Society, 9
Ammons, Eddie, mentioned, 30
Anderson, James D., historian, 5
Ansley, Clarke Fisher, 24
API Club, Black Women's group, 93
Apollo Theatre in Harlem, N. Y., 74
Archives, Piney Woods, 135
Arkansas, 26
Armstrong, Samuel C., 8–9, 25

Baldwin, W. D., 113
Baldwin, William Henry, 5

Ballard, Seth, the family of, 128
Band, girls, 69
Barksdoll, Evelyn, 123
Barwick brothers, 30
Barwick, Caline, 30
Barwick, Homer, of Braxton, 112
Baseball team, 75, 114
Bass, Nellie, 79; Nellie Elaine Jones, 23, 47
Basutoland, Leribe, Cooperative Union in, 121
Bell Pine, 16, 47, 111
Bender, Lucille, 136
Berry, George, 123
Bible camps, 80
Bilmyer, Rebecca, 23
Bilbo, Senator Theodore G., wife of, 44
Blacks, 3, 5, 10, 15–16, 139; black and white relations, 113; community support, 34, 35; education, 8, 9, 11, 15, 34–35, 40, 41, 96, 133; black power, 114, 118, 134; black studies, 135; local 109
Blacksmith, 86
Blind colored students, 61, 62
Board of Education, 112–113
Boarding school, 7, 8, 67, 68, 78, 120
Bond, W. F., 68–69
Boy Scouts of America, 140
Braddy, Lenzie, 47, 71, 119
Braille Library curriculum, 83
Brandon, 48, 59, 126; bank of, 18; courthouse in, 18
Braxton, 14, 15–17, 30, 73; bank of, 35; high school of, 42; white folks of, 29, 112
Brethren Church, 80, 96, 113, 123
Brooks, Nellie F., 93
Brooks, Rose, 18, 52

163

Brown, A., 125-26
Brown, Edna Mae Taylor, 126
Brown, James E. D., 126
Building Commission of Mississippi, 85
Butterfield, Frances, 106
Byrd, Georgia, 35
Byrd, Joe E., 35

Campbell, Ed, 15
Campbell, Elijah, 17, 18, 36
Carney, Mabel, educator, 50
Carver, George Washington, scientists, 11, 26
Carter, Gertrude, 45, 49
Carter, Ernestine Pippins, 41, 126
Carter School of Brandon, 126
Carter, Ella Jane, 97, 98
Chaperons/matrons, 78-79
Chandler Auditorium, 102
Chandler, Zilpha Ellen, 93, 101, 102, 121
Chautauqua, 50
Chickasaw County, 51
Christmas, 52, 53, 54, 62; bundles 52; caroling, 111; gifts from Piney Woods, 107; holiday, 28; in Iowa tradition, 37; program for the blind, 82
Churubusco, Indiana, 96
Civil War, 14, 33, 96, 97
Civil Rights movement, 118
Cohay, sawmill, 16
Cole, Rev. Jessie, Iowa State Soldiers' Home, 93
College Park Auditorium, 85
Colored blind school, 80-85
Columbia University, 50, 98
Columbus, Ohio, 135
Columbus, Ohio school system, 134
Comby, 16, 18, 42; sawmill, 14, 30; post office, 35
Commencement Day, 86-87
Community, school, 67; spirit, 62; program, 137-138; folk, 36, 52, 53, 64; local 118
Community House, Jones's family home, 62
Complimenting, 79
Consolidation movement, 41, 119, 120
Cotton Blossom Singers, 69, 74, 97, 101, 113, 137; blind students, 83
Cox, Nellie Flowers, 18, 36, 52
Cox, Steve, 15, 36

Cox, J. P., 30
County agents, 46
County schools, 41, 69, 119, 120
County seat, 51
Crawford, Ed, 18
Crawford, Steven, 18
Crofton, Carrie S., 126
Crumpacker, Anna, 123
Curricula, 68-71, 120

Dar es Salaam, 121
Dansby, B. Baldwin, 116
Davis, Edna, 123
Day, Beth, 105
Dayton, C. L., 96
Deposit Guaranty Bank, 105, 139
Depression, 51, 67, 83, 97, 105
Des Moines, Iowa, 37, 91, 93, 94
Dickerman, G. S., with Slater Fund, 96
Dickman, Mrs., Upper Iowa University, 102
Dillard, James Hardy, 98
Dishman, Bertha, 64, 135
Discrimination among black students, 116-118
Dixie, people of, 112
Dixon, Bill, 32
Dixon family, 32
D'Lo Area, 26, 28, 29, 126, 127, 128
Donnell, Katie Catherine Love, 65, 66
Dormitories, 81; new boys, 138-139
Douglass, Frederick, 25
Dubois, W. E. B., 3, 25
Dulany, George W., 94-96
Dunbar Club, 130
Dunham, Melerson Guy, 60, 64

Early students, 64
East Africa, 121
Easter worship, 111
Education Department of Mississippi, 136
Education, Manual Labor, 3, 7, 8
Education, State Department of, 61, 69, 120
Edwards, Ralph, 105
Elementary Department at Piney Woods, 67
Eli Lilly Estate, 138
Elizabethtown College in Pennyslvania, 93
El Paso, Texas, Jones's father's home, 22

Ely, Mrs. of Mississippi Library Commission, 101
Episcopal Church, 22
Ethiopia, 120, 121
Europe, 7, 118, 123
Everett, R. F., 30, 35
Extension program, 42, 43, 44, 45, 46, 50, 51

Fair, community, 47, 50, 52, 115; Association of Piney Woods, 49
Fair, County, 140
Fair, Mississippi, 43, 137
Fair, New York's World's, 74
Fannin in Rankin County, 65
Farish Street Baptist Church, 52
Farm Agents, 40, 42, 118–119
Farmers' Conferences, 11, 42, 44, 50, 52, 115
Favrot, Leo M., 50
Federation of Colored Women's Clubs of Mississippi, 60, 61, 62, 64, 130
Federation of Women's Clubs, white, 61
Fellenberg, Phillip E. von, 7
Field Day, 62, 67
Finkbines, E. C., 94
Finkbines, W. O., 94
Finke, Olga, 69
First National Bank, 139
Fleischmann, Max, 106
Florence, Mississippi, 115, 127
Folk of the community, 36, 52, 53, 64
Folk traditions, 140
Ford Foundation, 121
Ford Motor Company, 138
Foreign visitors, 120
Forty acres for the school's beginning, 33
Foster, Prior, 8, 23–24, 36
Foster, Robert, 23
Four-H Clubs, 46, 140 (4-H Clubs)
Foxx, Martha Morrow, 80–85
Freedman's Bureau, 9
Fund raising, 35, 36

Gale, Rev. George W., 7
Galilee Baptist Church of Worth, West Virginia, 133
Gant, Mother, 78
Garfield, President, 31 (paraphrased)
General Education Board, 10, 97; Conference on Negro Education, 43

Gibson, Amon, 34, 35, 36, 37
Gilmore, Johnnie, 130–131
Girl Scouts of America, 140
Glee Club, 74, 112
Grace Memorial Club, 64
Gray, Lottie, mentioned, 32
Green Bay Lumber Company, 94
Greer, Rev. Chester A., 52
Gulf and Ship Island Railroad, 16

Haien, Jr., John, 133, 134, 136
Hall, George, 111
Halsey, Grace, 82
Hammill, Lee, 91
Hampton Institute, 5, 7, 8, 9, 24, 25, 81, 97, 98
Hardy, J. D., 46, 47, 48, 49, 71, 99
Harris, Montague, 15
Harris, Mordecai, 31
Hattiesburg, Mississippi, 123
Hayes, Reginald, 78
Hemphill, Bob, 29
Hicks, Green, 48
Hill, Forest, 132
Hilo Manuel Labor School for Hawaiians, 8
Hinds County, 26
Hobby, Jeannette James, 96
Holden, Prof. P. G., 44
Holtzclaw, Prof. William H., 11, 26
Home Demonstration Agent, 20, 45, 46, 118–119
Hooker, Calvin, 136–137
Hopkins, Mark, 25, 31
Hospitality House, mentioned, 106
Howard University, 97, 106
Howland, Emily, 91, 102
Hughes, Leola, 17, 20, 28, 31, 57
Huxford, J. H., 93
Hyde, A. A., 96

Illinois, 24, 123
Iowa, 22, 42, 127; financial support, 35, 36, 38, 91, 93; Jones's high school career there, 24
Iowa State University, 93
Indians, mentioned, 14
Industrial education, 3, 5, 10, 11–12, 24, 25, 30, 140, 141
Industrial Institutes, 5
Industrial Revolution, 7

Industrial School for delinquent boys, 61
Industrial technology, 5
Integration, 138
International Harvester, 49
Ishmael Jordon, former student, 132
Iowa City, Iowa, 55

Jack, Bettye Mae, 41, 132
Jackson State University, formerly college, 11, 52, 75, 101, 116, 137; library, 101
Jackson, Mississippi, 52, 66, 135
Jackson Prairie, part of Rankin County, 13
Jamestown Exposition, 25
Jazz Band, 74
Jeanes, Anna T. Jeanes Fund, 10, 40–41, 96, 98
Jeanes teachers, 40, 42, 126, 132
Jehovah's Witnesses, 126
Jessup, President of SUI, 102
Jim Crow, 11, 96, 107, 111, 114
Johnson, Bertha L., educator, 11, 61
Johnson, J. E., 11
Johnson, Sr., Paul B., Governor, 61, 84
Johnson, Selby, 93
Jones, Flora Mae, Laurence Jones's sister, 23
Jones, Gabe local Braxton residence, 30
Jones, Grace Allen, 52–53, 55–64, 74, 80, 97, 127, 130; her mother, 93
Jones, John, Laurence Jones's father, 22, 23
Jones, John Bernard, former Vice President of Development, 137
Jones, Laurence Clifton, 3, 7, 8, 11, 15, 20; early life in St. Joseph, Missouri, 22–24; high school and college in Iowa 24–26; at Utica Institute, 26; founding of Piney Woods School, 11, 26–36; Piney Woods folks, 28; encouraged blacks to stay in the South, 44; student work, 65, 67; community fair, 49; managed normal school, 69; seeking support for the school, 91–108 *passim*; nature of relationship with whites, 109, 110; life in jeopardy, 110–111; black contemporary opinion of, 116; on unemployment, 119; student protest, 135; *passim*
Jones, Laurence C., Foundation, 138

Jones, Jr., Laurence Clifton, second son of Laurence and Grace Jones, 62
Jones, Mary Foster, mother of L. C. Jones, 23
Jones, Nellie, (Hardy, Bass), L. C. Jones's baby sister, 23, 47, 79
Jones, Ruby Ethel, sister of L. C. Jones, 23
Jones, Turner, first son of L. C. and Grace Jones, 62
Junior Achievement, 140
Junior College at Piney Woods, 69, 120, 129, 130–131

Kay, Virginia of Los Angeles, 106
Keller, Helen, 84, 114
Kenya, 121
Keokuk, Iowa, 33, 91
King, Arena C. Mallory, educator, 11
Kirkland, Madeline, educator, 106
Korean War, 127

Laboratory school, Piney Woods, 119
Land Grant Act of 1890, 40
Land grant colleges, 40, 43
Lattimore, Alice, 74
Laurence C. Jones Foundation, 138
Lee of Oakley Neal Cafe, 48
Lee, Robert E., 46, 48, 49
Leuthold, Blanche Dulany, 106
Liberal arts tradition, 3, 7
Liberty loan campaigns, 51
Library commission, 101
Lichty, D. Eugene and Eloise, 113–114
Loess Hills, part of Rankin County, 13
Log cabin, 17, 18, 20, 32, 33, 34, 36, 42, 62
Lundford, Andy, 18
Lunky, Aunt, ex-slave, 94; storage for donated items, 52, 135
Lutheran mission, 79, 123
Lutheran Synodical Conference, 79
Lynching, 103

Machobane Mass Agricultural College, 121
Maddox, Ralph, Superintendent of Simpson County Schools, 35
Madison, County, 18
Maltbie, Milo, Upper Iowa University, 102

Mangum, Wiley P., 29, 30, 37
Manchester Church of Brethren College, 96
Manual labor education, 3, 7, 8
Marshalltown (Iowa) High School, 24
Martin, Mary E., 37, 41
Marysville, Missouri, 22
Masonic lodges, 11, 125
Matrons/chaperons, 78–79
Mause, Miss with Jackson School for the Blind, 83
McBryde, Mrs. S. A., 83
McCullough, B. T., 16
McDowell County, West Virginia, 133
McGee, Dr. Samuel, former Piney Woods administrator, 137
McKay, Will, of Braxton, 112
McLaurin, Alex, 15
McLaurin, Hector, 34, 35, 36
McLean, George E., former President of University of Iowa, 24, 93
McNeil, Don, Breakfast Show, 105
McPherson College, 126, 137
Mechanical Arts College, 40
Mendenhall, Mississippi, 42, 138; high school, 127; study club, 112
Meridian, 11
Methodist Church, 113
Mexicans, 117, 120
Michigan, Addison, 8
Michigan Agricultural College, 8
Michigan State University, 8
Miller, E. B., Mrs., 130
Miller, Dr. L. T., 130
Millsaps, R. W., 106
Minnesota, student travel there, 127
Missionary groups, 9, 10
Mississippi, 73, 97, 99; black folk, 44, 45, 101
Mississippi Delta, 13–14, 16
Mississippi development, 44, 46
Mississippi Hall of Fame, 125
Mississippi Library Commission, 101
Mississippi State College, 46
Mississippi State Tuberculosis Sanitorium, 54, 61
Missouri, 26, 94
Moman, Eula Kelly, 123, 135
Montessori nursery, 69
Morrill Land Grant Acts, 10, 40
Mothers' Club, 36, 57–59, 60, 61, 62

Moton, Robert R. former president of Tuskegee, 61, 107
Mountain Grove Church of Brethren in Missouri, 113
Music program, 69
Muskhoff, Henry C., 96
Myers, 'Mot,' Superintendent of Rankin County Schools, 35

Natchez region, 14
National Club Women's movement, 57
National School Lunch Act, 99
National Youth Administration, 134
Negroes, 14–15, 107, 112, 113; education, 8, 9, 10, 11, 15, 20–21, 24, 25, 30, 34–35, 40, 41, 68–69, 96, 116, 133; teachers, 120
Negro spirituals, 74, 79, 86, 107
Neighborhood Youth Administration (NYA), 52, 99
New Deal, 119
New Hope County School field day, 62
Newton County, Mississippi, 47
North, 28, 115, 127
Northerners, 102, 109
Nyerere, Julius, President of Tanzania, 121

Oakley Training School, 61
Oberlin College, 7, 8
Ogden, Robert C., 5
Ohio, 23
O'Neal, Mr. and Mrs. K. R., 138
Oneida Presbyter, 7
Oral tradition, 14
Otis, J. R., President of Alcorn College, 124
Overbrook School for the Blind, 80, 81

Palmer, Superintendent of Marshalltown public schools, 93
Parish, Estella, 96, 107
Patterson, Frederick, D., 98
Pattie, Roy, mentioned, 30
Peabody, George Foster, 5, 96–97, 98
Peabody Education Fund, 10, 97
Peacock, Dorothy of Charleston, Mississippi, 130
Pearl River Counties, 14
Pestalozzi, Johann Heinrich, Swiss educator, 7
Phelps, Bill, 110

Phelps-Stokes Fund, 10
Phifer, Claude, 68, 130
Philanthropic agencies, 9
Philanthropists, 5, 9, 97
Pine Grove Baptist Church of D'Lo, 128
Pine Torch, 102–103, 141
Piney Woods Alumni Association, 128
Piney Woods Endowment, 105
Piney Woods Post Office, 105
Piney Woods region, 13–14
Pioneer Bible Camps, 80
Pippins, Ernestine (Carter), 41, 126
Plummer, James deJornette, 123
Polk, Deborah Gray, 20, 62
Practical learning, 69–74
Prentiss Normal and Industrial Institute, 11, 40, 61, 75, 78
Price, Beatrice, 130
Protest, 118
Pruitt, Anderson, 30
Public schools, 41, 61
Public Welfare Department, 83

Quilting, 20
Quilting parties, 58

Racial harmony, 111, 109–116
Racial segregation, 132
Rankin County, 13, 18, 21, 22, 29, 35, 45, 46, 47, 50, 59, 80, 99, 101, 114, 118, 120, 125, 126, 128
Rankin County 4-H Clubs, 46
Rays of Rhythm, 69, 74
"Rap-Jacking," boys' game, 75–76
Red Cross, American, 51, 59
Reese, Everett, Chairman of Piney Woods School Board, 134
Religion, 55; instruction, 5, 62, 78–80
Retirement system of Piney Woods, 135
Robbins, R. C., 132
Robertson, Smith, 126–27
Rockefeller, John D., 10, 82
Rosenwald Foundation, Julius, 10, 67, 98
Rosenwald School at Piney Woods, 67, 96, 99, 119
Ross, Lennie Feazell, 62
Rural blacks, 3, 12, 50, 125, 139
Rural education, 11, 22, 42, 50, 69, 130
Rural School Improvement Association, 38, 42
Rust College, 52, 98

Saints Junior College, 11
Sanders, Joseph, 130
Sawmill, 16–17, 29
Schmidt, G. A., Rev., Lutheran minister, 79
School closing, 36, 37, 38
Scott County, 21, 41, 132
Segregation, 111; schools, 22
Skills, 3, 38, 69
Simpson County, 15, 17, 18, 21, 35, 41, 42, 47, 50, 98, 101, 118, 119, 126, 128
Slater Fund, John F., 10, 41, 43, 67, 96, 97, 98
Slimmer, Abraham, 94; Slimmer Endowment Foundation, 105
Smart, Robert J., 130
Smith County, 21, 101
Smith-Hughes Act, 10, 43, 46; teachers, 43
Smith-Hughes boys section of fair, 49
Smith-Lever Act, 10, 43, 45
Smith, Olivia H., 52
Social life, 68, 76–79
South, 13, 24, 44, 103, 112; rural, 40
South Africa, 121
South Rhodesia, 121
Southern Association of Colleges and Schools, 136
Southern Education Board Conference, 96
Southern hospitality, 108
Southerners, 102, 135; whites, 109, 112, 114
Sports at Piney Woods, 74–76
Standard Brand Securities, 106
State Board of Development, 49
State Department of Education, 50, 61, 69, 120
State Legislature, 101
St. John's Church, 28
St. Joseph, Missouri, 22; High School, 24
Students, description of, 38–39
Summer school, 68, 120
Superstitions, 54–55, 59–60
Sweethearts of Rhythm, 69, 74

"Talented tenth", 3
Talladega, 97–98
Tanzania, 121, 141
Taylor, Edward Nelson, 18, 32–34, 35, 52, 86, 91; Hall 36

Index 168

Taylor, Nathan, 15
Thanksgiving, 52, 74
Third World, 141
"This Is Your Life," 105
Thrift stamp campaigns, 51; clubs, 134
Tougaloo College, 11, 18, 34, 52, 101
Training schools, 43
Trustees of Piney Woods School, 33, 109, 134, 135, 138
Tuition at Piney Woods School, 73, 74
Tulane University, 41
Turner, Capt. and Mrs. Asa, 42, 44, 91, 110
Turner, Marvel, vice-president for business affairs, 137
Tuskegee Institute, 11, 24, 25, 26, 61, 98, 123; Alumni Association, 128
Tuskegee-Piney Woods tradition, 126

Uganda, 121
Underground railroad, 23
Underprivileged, 130, 139; bottom rail of society, 3, 139, 140
Uniforms, 66–67, 76
United War Fund, 51
University of Iowa, 24, 26, 91–93, 94
Utica Institute, 11, 26, 28, 40, 75, 78, 98, 126, 127

Vardaman, James, former governor, 21
Vocational training, 5
Volunteers, 9, 13, 123, 135

Wade, James S., background, 113–134; first days at Piney Woods, 134–135; administration, 132, 134–138; comments on Piney Woods today, 137; changes in school program, 138
Warren, Mary E. G. Thomas, 136, 137
Washington, Booker T., 3, 11, 25, 26, 73, 97, 98, 106, 107
Watkins, Mary Parker, 117
Watson, Louis, 37, 52
Weathersby, Forten, 26, 29, 52, 126; family of, 126–128; Eva, 28, 126; Milton, 119, 127–128; Pauline Y., 127; S. P., Sr., 127; S. P., Jr., 128; Syntyche Carola, 128; Milton Vanzetti II, 128
Weathersby, Docia, 31, 37
Weathersby, Early, 32
Weathersby, Jack, 32
Weathersby, Lessie, 31
Weathersby, Mary, 32
Weaver, Willie of Atlanta, Georgia, 130
Webb, T. K. of Florence, Mississippi, 115
Webb, John L., 61
Webster, John R., 14–15, 18, 29, 30, 35, 109, 110
Weddell, Rev. Erwin R., 80
Welfare system, 84, 119, 139
Western Reserve Theological Seminary, 7
Whites of Piney Woods community, 4, 14–16, 29, 35, 53, 109, 111, 112, 115–116, 124
William, Pattie, 30
Wilson, J. C., 51
Wilson, R. S., 44
Wilson, Woodrow, Piney Woods graduate, 129–130
Wolfer, Sue Riley, 93
Women's concerns in the Piney Wood area, 57–64
Women's Clubs, Federated Colored, 80
Woodstock Manual Labor Institute, 8, 23
Work program at Piney Woods, 67, 68
Work ethic and jobs, 73–74
World War I, 50, 59, 60, 110
World War II, 75, 124, 125, 127
Wright, Fielding, 85

Yancy, William F., 31, 34, 37
Yazoo City, Mississippi, 130
Young Men's Christian Association, 80, 140
Young Women's Christian Association, 62, 80, 140
Zimmerman, Attorney, A. A., 91

www.ingramcontent.com/pod-product-compliance
Lightning Source LLC
Chambersburg PA
CBHW030344240426
43661CB00052B/1738